DATE DUE

~~DE~~		
~~OCT 6 01~~		
~~MY 18 02~~		
~~DE 2 02~~		
~~AP 29 03~~		
~~MY 20 '03~~		
~~JY 31 '06~~		

Letters to Kennedy

LETTERS
TO
KENNEDY

John Kenneth Galbraith

Edited by JAMES GOODMAN

HARVARD UNIVERSITY PRESS

Cambridge, Massachusetts

London, England

1998

Library of Congress Cataloging-in-Publication Data

Galbraith, John Kenneth, 1908–
Letters to Kennedy / John Kenneth Galbraith ; edited by James Goodman.
p.   cm.
Includes index.
ISBN 0-674-52837-9 (cloth : alk. paper)
1. Kennedy, John F. (John Fitzgerald), 1917–1963—Correspondence.
2. Galbraith, John Kenneth, 1908–   —Correspondence.
3. United States—Politics and government—1961–1963.
4. United States—Foreign relations—1961–1963.
5. United States—Economic conditions—1961–1971.
6. Presidents—United States—Correspondence.
7. Economists—United States—Correspondence.
I. Goodman, James, 1956– . II. Title.
E842.A4 1998
973.922′092′2—dc21   97–38839

To remember
JFK

Contents

Letters to Kennedy

Introduction

It is now a third of a century and something more since these letters were written. The question arises as to why, the usual vanity of authors apart, they should now be published. The answer, one often too easily offered, is that history has its claims. This was an interesting, even exciting time on the American and larger world scenes. The letters come if not precisely from the center of that stage, at least from a position of considerable advantage. But there is a further claim.

John F. Kennedy was an extraordinarily intelligent person. He was also a prodigious reader and far from uncritical in his reactions. Accordingly, he commanded from his correspondents a strong effort in any written communication; there was always the thought that anything dull, profuse, too obviously self-serving, would be quickly and perhaps not quietly discarded. He did not suffer fools gladly nor did he suffer bad prose. There were diverse matters on which I needed to inform him, or at least I so thought. On no writing have I ever lavished so much attention. Frequently over a lifetime I have sought, not wholly without success, to write for a substantial audience. Reflecting on these letters, I am led to say that possibly some of my better writing, certainly some of my most attentive writing, was for an audience of one. That, to be sure, is my view; the less personal, more detached reaction I leave to the critics.

These letters are divided between politics, economics, and foreign policy, with particular emphasis on the bearing of the latter on the Asian subcontinent, extending from Pakistan to Vietnam. They reflect the mood and issues of those years.

In economics they present the liberal post-Keynesian view, tempered as always by what seemed politically acceptable and appealing.

As is made clear, I had differences with some of the other major sources of economic advice at the time. In a day of strong unions, strong employers, and a persistent threat of wage-price inflation, I was deeply committed to government pressure for restraint by both unions and employers. This was accepted by Kennedy; for some of his advisers the free market with prices controlled only by fiscal and monetary action was sufficient. Unemployment, the modern instrument against inflation, had not yet become an acceptable design.

There was another solid difference with my economic colleagues: with revenues strong and the budget deficit no longer a central issue, they were for cutting taxes in order, they hoped, to stimulate yet greater economic growth. (Tax cuts simply for the sake of not paying taxes were not, as now, a confessed motivation.) I strongly preferred an increase in expenditures for urgent social purposes, especially for the poor. I did, I think, delay the eventual decision, but by the time of Kennedy's murder I was on the losing side. The tax cut came in the early months of the next administration.

The greatest number of these letters deal with foreign policy and, not surprisingly, with India. (Some, I should note, were published earlier in the journal that I kept in those years.) The context, which is not without continuing relevance, calls for a special word.

An ambassador is both the representative of the president and an extended arm of the State Department. This dual and, in my case, conflicting role was a controlling factor in more than a few of these letters. It is still an important and poorly understood fact in foreign relations.

Most agencies of the United States government enforce legislation, administer programs. This is the case with the Departments of Agriculture, Labor, and Transportation, and, even to some extent, the Pentagon. The State Department, in contrast, and with some exceptions, administers policy. Policy then becomes belief. Instructions as they flow out, action when it is required, are the expression of the accepted policy. To this policy all are expected to adhere. In the absence of such a commitment there would, indeed, be chaos. But, with rare exceptions, those who thus administer policy come not only to accept it but to believe in it. Were it otherwise, they would live in daily, hourly conflict with themselves, and they would not be thought effective in their role. In the most telling expression, the individual so motivated would not be a good soldier. The problem arises when the policy must be changed, when it is wrong or obsolete, for belief in it persists. So it was in the Kennedy years. The policy, the belief, that had been inherited came from an earlier time, and especially that of John Foster Dulles and at least symbolically his brother Allen, the head of the CIA, known to some of us as the duller Dulles.

The policy so translated into belief centered, needless to say, on the Cold War and Communism, and on Communism's threat to the Third World. Here India was the centerpiece and Indochina, particularly Vietnam, the area of clear and present threat. A major component of this policy was a string of military alliances—NATO and on to SEATO, CENTO, ANZUS—which brought together the Middle Eastern and Asian countries and extended to Australia and New Zealand and by inference to the islands of the Pacific. India stood apart from and rejected these alliances. In the elementary but far from unimportant policy belief, it was thus available to either side.

I had long thought that Communism was not a viable threat in the Third World—that before you could have Communism, there had to be capitalism and that in a poor peasant society (or a Vietnam jungle) both were irrelevant. To this view the State Department most assuredly did not subscribe. Here the controlling role of belief. What had become policy over the Dulles years had become the accepted and acceptable belief. To this, with a few exceptions, the new Kennedy arrivals then subscribed, and especially Dean Rusk, the secretary of state. (So did Phillips Talbot, the assistant secretary for my part of the world.) Chester Bowles, the new under secretary of state, was an ardent spokesman for my general position. He was very soon sacked, which in Washington often means being moved upward to some totally functionless and anonymous post.

There is always danger as well as pleasure in exaggerating one's own role in history; nothing, in consequence, is so rightly suspect. Still, with the departure of Bowles, I became one of the few voices for a rational non-militarist policy toward the Third World and, needless to say, India and Vietnam. This was the background of a number of these letters.

It was essential, I thought, that my communications go directly to the White House; in the State Department they would merely stagnate under the weight of the accepted belief. Not liking this access to the president, Secretary Rusk asked McGeorge Bundy, Kennedy's national security advisor, to have my letters go through the Department. Kennedy, who had told me and others that he liked them, asked what I thought. In a resort to a kind of metaphor that should be used sparingly, I replied that "communicating through the Department would be like fornicating through the mattress." The direct communication continued.

There was, of course, more. During these years there was the brief border war between China and India, which, more than incidentally, put in doubt my position as to Communist intentions in the Third World. It coincided with the missile crisis in Cuba and in the more alarmed view—that of Secretary Rusk in particular—was part of the Communist strategy in the larger world. For the moment my own convictions were modestly shaken. But within a few days the war emerged as a less than cosmic dispute over some distant and desolate landscape, which, exceptionally among Americans or Europeans, I had actually visited. (In a much later conversation with Rajiv Gandhi, who was then in negotiation with China over the same territory, I said, though not solemnly, that one could only wish that it might belong to someone else.) The Chinese offered a cease-fire. Hearing of it, I arose early that morning to urge Prime Minister Nehru to accept it; this, rather gratefully, he did. He did not wish for any more war, and especially one in which the Indian military establishment had shown itself to be sadly defective. The Soviet ambassador told me that they were as happy as we to see the hostilities come to an end.

There are historical references and explanations in the endnotes which extend well beyond the letters that are the basic core of the book. Nearly all of these are the work of my intelligent and accomplished editor; occasionally I added a few words, but the major credit belongs to him.

I

Politics

Harvard University
Cambridge, Massachusetts
August 25, 1959

Mr. Harold Hayes
Articles Editor
Esquire
488 Madison Avenue
New York, N.Y.

Dear Mr. Hayes:

This is in reply to your letter of August 6.[1] It was greatly delayed reaching me. I am happy to respond.

I am supporting my good friend and fellow Massachusetts Democrat, Senator John F. Kennedy for the Democratic Nomination and needless to say for election.

As to the issues, I would think there are four. The first is to find some durable alternative to the present strategy of deterence with which we can live in greater safety. The second, is to find some way of assisting the poor lands which takes account not only of their need for capital but also the urgent pressures for political and social advancement. Thirdly, we must find some way of reconciling price stability with full employment and economic growth. Fourth and finally, we must correct the notable disparity between our comparative private opulence and the poverty of our public services.

All would seem to me a sufficient assignment for the next President.

Yours faithfully,
J. K. Galbraith

September 11, 1959

Professor J. K. Galbraith
Harvard University
Cambridge, Massachusetts

Dear Ken:

Just a note to express a double word of gratitude—both for your epistle to *Esquire* and for a copy of your most recent diary.[2]

I hope that your entry in *Esquire* will not be a piece of solitary wisdom, though I rather imagine that your voice will be drowned out by the antiphonal choruses of support for Pat Brown, Soapy Williams and Bob Wagner![3] Nonetheless, I am very grateful.

I regret that my days in Conference with Graham Barden and Phil Landrum[4] did not permit me to snatch hours in which to read your impressions of the U.S.S.R. There were times when I would have liked to take your diary to the Conference in order to give the hours greater buoyancy. However, I was afraid that you might be laid open to withering attacks by Mr. Landrum and that you might join Drew Pearson's portrait gallery along with Archie Cox.[5] Therefore, I resisted the temptation. I shall take it along with me on my first journey after we fold our tents on Capitol Hill. I only hope that on arriving in Columbus, Ohio, I will be treated better than you apparently were in Alma Ata.[6]

I hope that we can get together in the reasonably near future, and take some soundings on the future.

With every good wish,

Sincerely,
John F. Kennedy

Harvard University
Cambridge, Massachusetts
December 17, 1959

Senator John F. Kennedy
United States Senate Office Building
Washington, D.C.

Dear Jack:

Notice what happens when an egghead bites Kennedy. However, I take it this means you're in.[7]

More seriously, I have a feeling that the whole upshot of the birth control business hasn't been too bad. I can't think that this sort of thing is ever very helpful, but in the last few days, I have heard quite a few people attacking the President's stand more than yours. Also, I would guess that Mrs. Roosevelt helped.[8]

May I wish you as pleasant a Christmas as the present state of tension allows.

Yours faithfully,
J. K. Galbraith

Enc. 12/17 issue of *Crimson*

Harvard University
Cambridge, Massachusetts
June 1, 1960

Senator John F. Kennedy
United States Senate Office Building
Washington, D.C.

Dear Jack:

This is to let you know that I am back in town again, although I can't see that you are in any serious need of anything.[9] I must say, watching the primary campaigns from a distance, they gave me an impression of a brilliant as well as professional operation and deserving of the results achieved.

I also noticed coming back after three or four months a marked shift in the egghead attitude. Indeed, I have even collected some mild acclaim for my advanced perception. I would gather this to mean that intellectuals, like others, are subject to the bandwagon effect or, hopefully, have an eye for a winner.

Yours faithfully,
J. K. Galbraith

P.S. I have just had a call from Chayes to say that Ted is coming to town.[10] JKG

Harvard University
Cambridge, Massachusetts
July 16, 1960

Senator John F. Kennedy
Hyannis Port, Massachusetts

Dear Jack:

I hesitate to add to all the comment, liturgical and otherwise, you will have had on the acceptance speech. I listened to it here in Cambridge.[11] But there are two matters which concern the future which I venture to bring up.

Let me say that I greatly approved the content. The New Frontier theme struck almost exactly the note that I had hoped for in my memorandum.[12] So did the low key references to defense and Mr. K.[13] The reference to religion was good and indeed moving. By its nature much of the speech had to be an exercise in rhetoric, an art form in which I have never found it possible to practice, but it safely negotiated the delicate line that divides poetry from banality. I would hope that you would not need soon again to return to religion. You *could* succeed in making this an issue by speaking on it more frequently than is absolutely necessary. And your references to it are a license for others.

My suggestions concern construction of the speech itself—or rather those ahead. In the first place, your speech last night was essentially unfinished. It was badly in need of editing and polish. As a purely literary matter, the sentences could have been greatly smoothed. The images could have been much sharper and more vivid. Some superfluous words could have been drained out. The transitions could have been far smoother and more skillful. Your small transitions and changes of pace were insufficiently marked off from your major ones. This is partly a matter of speaking. But it is much more one of working into the text the warnings and signals (both to you and the audience) of the changes to come. Last night you were often well into the next sequence before the audience had realized that you had left the last. However, I do not wish to stress this point to the exclusion of others. The sharpening of images and allusions is also very important. All these matters not only make the speeches more effective. But they also make them much *much* easier to give.

I hope that this won't be taken as criticism of anyone who worked on the speech. I am aware of the pressure. And this problem of editing was (in my judgment) the most serious one we had in the Stevenson campaigns.[14] It wasn't always possible to persuade people of the need. Adlai himself was a very deft editor but especially in 1956 he did not have the time. In that year Willard Wirtz[15] functioned as editor but ended up rewriting all speeches, a wholly different and quite ruinous thing. (This was the principal reason the 1956 speeches were inferior to those of 1952.) A part of the problem of editing is merely good planning—to have the speeches in draft and generally approved in time for polishing and the rest.

My next point concerns the nature of the speeches. It is evident that in straightforward exposition and argument you are superb. On the basis of your Los Angeles performances—before the caucuses and in dealing with Lyndon—I am prepared to argue that you have few masters in your time. When it comes to oratorical flights and Stevenson-type rhetoric, you give a reasonable imitation of a bird with a broken wing. You do get off the ground but it's wearing on the audience to keep wondering if you are going to stay up.

The solution here is simple. You cannot avoid these flights into space entirely—they are part of our political ritual. And maybe you could be less self-consciously awful in their performance although personally I would be sorry if you were. But the real answer is to keep this part of the speechmaking to the absolute minimum. My own guess is that people will welcome matter-of-fact and unpretentious discussion and anyhow that is what won you the primaries. In any case, I don't think you have a choice.

I hope this doesn't sound too much like Baruch.[16] It was damaging to have the people around the headquarters in Los Angeles calling me Sir.[17]

Do have a good rest—this would seem to me more important than anything else.

Sincerely,

J. K. Galbraith

P.S. I am leaving to go up to Newfane this afternoon and for a few days my secretary here will be on vacation. I think your secretary must have my Vermont number which is Forest 5–7582. This, indeed, would be the best for any time in the next few weeks.

July 29, 1960

Senator John F. Kennedy
Hyannis Port, Massachusetts

Dear Jack:

Nixon's claim to vast experience in a period of trouble and peril is going to be one of our most difficult and perhaps our most difficult issue. And clearly, noticing Dewey[18] and others, the word has been passed that this is to be it. The claim could get away from us and keep the campaign on the defensive. I don't think it can be met by subtleties. We must hit back directly. The Throttlebottom image of the vice-presidency must be stressed.[19] One does far less there than as a working Senator and this must be stressed and repeated. And similarly that Nixon's responsibilities were largely fabricated for the purpose of giving him prestige; that, as every sensible American must know, he has spent most of the last four years on his political career; that one does not learn how to deal with Khrushchev by talking with him for a few minutes in a kitchen; that Kennedy is an experienced member of the Foreign Relations Committee—something I have heard no one mention. There is a limit to what you personally can do along this line, of course. But I think it of prime importance that everyone else be alerted along these lines. Left to themselves, our people love to give statesmanlike speeches which elevate their own stature but don't strike where it is needed. The Republicans are far better at unity on a theme.

The papers seem to be making something of my role as an economic adviser. Needless to say, I have done nothing to encourage it. My line is that it can't be a very taxing job; it allows one to be absent for several months at a time in Switzerland.

Yours faithfully,
J. K. Galbraith

P.S. A leading British economist has just passed on a thought which I would like strongly to endorse. Don't be budged from your position that if we are going to have the things we need, we *may* have to have increased taxes. There is a perfectly good argument to the contrary—that it can be paid from the revenue from growth—but people simply don't believe it. The consequence is the worst tag of all—that of irresponsibility. Gaitskell's promise of greatly improved public services and no increase in taxes was, it is now agreed, a major campaign blunder.[20] JKG

Harvard University
Cambridge, Massachusetts
September 11, 1960

Senator John F. Kennedy
Los Angeles, California

Dear Jack:

I am here for a money-raising soiree at Henry Fonda's. I have some relaxed thoughts on the campaign and the issues which I would happily contribute. However, I want neither to break in on a needed relaxation nor thwart my ambition to be the most reticent adviser in modern political history.[21]

Yours faithfully,
John Kenneth Galbraith

September 27, 1960

Senator John F. Kennedy
United States Senate Office Building
Washington, D.C.

Dear Jack:

I am sorry I didn't get your call until just before the debate.[22]
I was in San Diego with Jackson, Ziffren, Yarborough[23] et al. at
the unemployment, social security conference.

I thought you were simply superb. I heard you on radio in a
Negro shoe shine parlor and asked the proprietor how *he* liked it.
He said, "So help me God, ah'm digging up two from the graveyard
for that boy." I was glad to see religion coming constructively into
the campaign.

Regards,
J. K. Galbraith

November 9, 1960

Telegram
President-Elect John F. Kennedy
Hyannis Port, Massachusetts

Special note to secretary: Please rescue from the pile. With your
highly developed sense of history, trust you will note that you are
the first presidential candidate since Truman to survive our support.
Warm and affectionate congratulations. May we arrange with
Reuther and Bowles for orderly transfer of Democratic Party to
your leadership?[24]

John Kenneth Galbraith

Arthur M. Schlesinger, Jr.[25]

November 10, 1960

PERSONAL
President-Elect John F. Kennedy
Hyannis Port, Massachusetts

Dear Jack*:

There has been talk in the Boston papers, and now this morning in *The New York Times,* that I am a prospect for your Senate seat. Without suggesting that this discussion has any serious substance, may I say that I am not a candidate for anything. Might I add, what I trust you know, that I would like to number myself among those of your friends and supporters who are sufficiently rewarded by being precisely that.[26]

I keep seeing in the papers what the South did for us. I wish someone would draw attention to the support we had from the poorer voters of the industrial north.

Yours faithfully,
J. K. Galbraith

* May I defer more seemly formality until the electoral college meets? Incidentally, deep in your pile of telegrams are my heartfelt congratulations.   JKG

January 9, 1961

Dear Mr. President:

Here is a further draft of the Inaugural which incorporates the changes you suggested at Palm Beach and numerous others.[27] I have had the help of Arthur and Walt Rostow,[28] and the part on disarmament toward the end is based on a draft by Walt. Let me make and stress these points.

(1) This is preeminently a speech for those who will read it rather than those who will hear it. The immediate audience will not long remember. The readers will render the ultimate decision. So, rightly I believe, I have made few concessions to your speaking style.

(2) I think, however, it is reasonably in character. My notion was to disavow pretentiousness but then maintain a reasonably even

and elegant flow of ideas. A few things—Walpurgis, the age of plain speaking, the three-toed sloth—are there as attention pieces. (The newspapers will promptly do research on sloths and German mythology.)

(3) I assume numerous further changes and amendments. Without proposing myself for added labor—my political life is ingloriously identified with a typewriter in a bathroom—I would happily take a hand in smoothing and unifying the tone of the final draft if you wish. The difference between a brilliant speech and a good one—at least of this sort—is what happens to it in the last half hour.

(4) The substance reflects, I believe, your general mood. On Latin America I discovered that Ike had once proposed the policy of the "Good Partner." After consideration and some discussion with the experts I have concluded that the right course is to build on the Roosevelt foundation,[29] which is presently your major advantage. Hence the present form.

(5) The conclusion I suppose must evoke God on some rising note. My secular talents do not extend so far. And no man can write another's prayers.

My best wishes. In case none gets used I will save a copy for 1964. We must strive for efficiency on the New Frontier.

Yours faithfully,
J. K. Galbraith

February 13, 1961

Dear Mr. President:

Here are some weekend thoughts:

(1) I haven't been much enchanted by this trip of Arthur Goldberg's.[30] Obviously one doesn't learn anything by visiting unemployed families in Detroit that isn't known or cannot otherwise be learned. So it is a gimmick and a slightly transparent one that makes capital out of misfortune. I suggest that after all of these years of Eisenhower, the rule should be: *Nothing Contrived, Nothing Bogus.* And nothing is so important as your reputation for playing it straight.

(2) I think it might be worthwhile quietly to caution top members

of the Administration against predicting a business upturn. (I have seen two or three optimistic statements in recent days.) No one really knows. If anything is certain, it is that one cannot talk business into a recovery. And nothing brings more discredit than promises of recovery à la Hoover that do not materialize.

(3) I sense that you are tapering off on the live television. This I would strongly endorse. If the taped performances could be spaced out, this too would be fine. My notion is that television exposure must be rationed for maximum effect. The time will doubtless come when you will need such effect.

(4) Economic and business comment on the economic and balance-of-payments messages has, I think, been favorable. Their moderation is taken as reassuring proof that my influence has been slight.

(5) Is someone riding herd on the Departments to make sure that *all* the promised legislation is getting up to the Hill promptly?

Yours faithfully,
J. K. Galbraith

Washington
March 16, 1961

Memorandum for the President
From: John Kenneth Galbraith
Subject: Baruch

An assignment which you gave me during the campaign at the suggestion of Mrs. Roosevelt—and conceivably forgotten by you in the trivial developments since—was to look after Bernard Baruch.[31] This I have done with incomparable diligence. I have had a several hour talk with him in New York (following which you wrote him a letter) and, at appropriate weekly intervals since, we have had long telephone discussions on the economic prospect or absence thereof. As the result of my efforts, he did not endorse Nixon although he may have been very, very slightly influenced by the thought that Mr. Nixon might not win.

Anyhow, I wonder if you shouldn't drop the old boy a note and invite him in. This will be in a great presidential tradition although in a greater tradition he often invited himself. You will see the best looking man of ninety in the entire land; you will observe a vanity that equals anything you have encountered even in the United States Senate; and you will make him very happy. Also, you will henceforth be a part of Bernard Baruch's four cylinder, triple-expansion, high altitude, ultra-high frequency name dropping by which I am totally and utterly fascinated. My favorite example: "I said, 'Josepheus, I want to tell you right here in front of Woodrow that your boy Franklin has a lot of the stuff. I think he is another comer like this English fellow Winston Churchill. Oliver agrees with me and so does Louis.'"

I attach a possible note.

Attachment

March 16, 1961

Mr. Bernard Baruch
597 Madison Avenue
New York City, New York

Dear Mr. Baruch:

Ken Galbraith has told me several times of his talks with you. I would very much like to see you one day at your convenience—perhaps you could stop when you are coming through Washington from South Carolina. The economic situation is giving me a good deal of concern and I would especially appreciate your thoughts on this.

Do let me know when you are likely to be in Washington.

Sincerely yours,

March 22, 1961

The Honorable John Kenneth Galbraith
The White House
Washington, D.C.

My dear Mr. Ambassador:

I have received with pleasure your recent communication sent at the inspiration of several senior members of the Cosmos Club.[32]

You are perhaps the first commentator to place me in the same intellectual firmament with President William Howard Taft. This is in itself no inconsiderable distinction. However, the knowledge that Presidents Wilson and Hoover were other links in this scholarly dynasty encourages me to respond favorably to your suggestion of membership. I would hope that my membership would not imply my attendance at scheduled meetings or at lectures. With the understanding that my participation in the activities of the Cosmos Club would be at best episodic, I accept with pleasure the invitation which President Conant and the Ambassador to India have tendered to me.

With best thanks,

Sincerely,
John F. Kennedy

November 9, 1961

Dear Mr. President:

At your request, I have gone over the Department of Defense draft pamphlet called "Fallout Protection—What to Know About Nuclear Attack—What to Do About It." I must tell you that I have read this document with grave misgiving, though not without realization of the serious problems moral and political which the whole issue involves.[33]

It is evident first of all that we will be seriously criticized if we seem not to be taking sensible precautions. And we would be morally delinquent if people died in a catastrophe when they might be saved by our foresight. However, there is a right and a wrong way to discharge our responsibilities and this pamphlet represents, I fear, the wrong way. I have five specific objections, as follows:

1. The pamphlet does not make clear that it is American policy to avoid a holocaust. Civilian defense represents contingency planning, with the word contingency strongly underlined. As a government we hope and indeed intend to save our people from this disaster. This is not made clear in the present pamphlet.

2. The present pamphlet is a design for saving Republicans and sacrificing Democrats. These are the people who have individual houses with basements in which basement or lean-to fallout shelters can be built. There is no design for civilians who live in wooden three deckers, tenements, low cost apartments, or other congested areas. I am not at all attracted by a pamphlet which seeks to save the better elements of the population, but in the main writes off those who voted for you. I think it particularly injudicious, in fact it is absolutely incredible, to have a picture of a family with a cabin cruiser saving itself by going out to sea. Very few members of the UAW can go with them.

3. The rest of the social philosophy underlying this pamphlet is equally offensive. While maintenance of an Army and Navy and their protection in case of an attack are well recognized functions of the State, the protection of the civilian is herewith assigned to private enterprises. This is on the theory that the civilian is too expensive a luxury to protect. The pamphlet even makes a virtue of this by saying: 'The anticipation of a new market for home shelters is helpful and in keeping with the free enterprise way of meeting changing conditions in our lives.'

All of this, of course, is related to the social discrimination in survival. We don't want to pay the price of deep urban shelters so we are writing off the slum dwellers.

4. I also worry a little bit about the effect on the Soviets of a great helter skelter shelter program such as this pamphlet could set off and with all the commercial publicity attached. Isn't this a rather ostentatious form of war preparation? I think we are also likely to set off a certain amount of racketeering on people's fears.

5. Finally, and perhaps a minor point, it seems to me that the pamphlet is extremely sanguine, both about life in the shelter and the world into which people emerge. The latter will be a barren and hideous place with no food, no transportation and full of stinking

corpses. Perhaps this can't be said but I don't think the people who wrote this pamphlet quite realize it.

Recommendations

1. This pamphlet should not be broadcast in its present form. I would consider it a minor disaster if this were done.
2. No shelter program can be cheap. If a decision is taken to initiate such a program, "do it yourself" recommendations for the comparatively well to do must be matched by public outlays on behalf of those who cannot afford shelters.
3. Accordingly we must decide that when and if a shelter program is launched it will be for *all* the people. While it is a hard decision I would not presently support such a democratic shelter program. The incredible cost and the effect on the Soviets are the factors.
4. The foregoing means this pamphlet should be radically revised.
   a) It should make clear that it represents contingency planning and that the prime purpose of hope is still pinned on the avoidance of nuclear disaster and that we expect to succeed. This must receive major stress.
   b) It should tell, as this pamphlet interestingly does, of the facts about fallout distribution, radiation, burns, blasts, first aid, etc.
   c) I come now to a choice:
      (1) If it is technically possible to say something important and useful about inexpensive protection in the event of nuclear attack for the tenement dwellers, the persons in the multiple apartment houses, in congested areas of the city and the like, then it might be possible also to tell what the more fortunately situated family could do. The pictures and text must be revised to stress the salvation of the poor. If nothing useful and detailed can be said along these lines then choice two becomes operative.

      We cannot tell the poor family in a big city which would like to live that the government has written it off. The present pamphlet if read by such a family without the space or the money for a shelter would cause it to conclude that its prospect was hopeless. It would alarm without giving hope.

(2) If nothing can usefully and honestly be said on behalf of dwellers in the congested areas, then the government cannot sponsor a "do it yourself" shelter program. It should say clearly that when in our judgment such a program is deemed necessary and essential it will be undertaken. The magnitude of that decision should be indicated by the magnitude of the cost, but it should also be made clear that there will be no shelter program that doesn't meet the needs of all of the people.

Sincerely,
John Kenneth Galbraith

New Delhi, India
January 23, 1962

Dear Mr. President:

In accordance with our conversation I got hold of John Oakes[34] for lunch, without of course his knowing that the suggestion had come from you. I thought this a time not for a barrage but for the one tough point, namely, that the *Times* is one hell of a lot harder on Kennedy for doing a lot but not enough than it was on Eisenhower for doing nothing or slightly less. For exceptional emphasis I made the same point three times with no variation.

He admitted the validity of the case—quite fully in fact. His first explanation was that there had been a change of administration at the *Times* as well as in Washington. I pointed out that, unlike the second change, the first was not known to the public at large. When he asked what I would urge, I suggested that he keep clearly before the public that they were criticizing a good Administration for its imperfections. This represented a vastly improved situation over the recumbent Administration which preceded. As usual, I had the feeling I was persuasive. This may be based largely on the fact that I persuaded myself.

I continue to feel, your annoyance notwithstanding, that we are better with the *Times* as it is than as it was. This will be further evidence that I reflect the inordinate perfectionism of American liberals.

I greatly enjoyed the visit on the plane the other morning. Things seem not to have deteriorated excessively in my absence and, as soon as I have cleared away the backlog, I am going to spend a few days on the beach completing the repairs of body and spirit and preparing for the rigors of the visit by your wife, of which I have now been adequately warned but which we are anticipating.

Yours faithfully,
John Kenneth Galbraith

Department of State
Washington
March 30, 1962

Dear Mr. President:

One thing I want to ask you about tomorrow on which you might require a moment's notice is Nixon's book.[35] I could do a thin scalpel job on this which by nuance and irony could be exceedingly destructive without giving anybody a handle for suggesting a partisan attack. The technique is to explore with great but lightly bogus sympathy why it is this good, good man goes through life being so persistently, terribly, and sadly misunderstood by so many, many people.

I can promise a devastating operation without any quotably adverse comment. He is ripe for this treatment and it could do damage for Nixon is just on the edge of being ridiculous and one could shove him over. On the other hand, there are obvious questions about my doing the job.

Yours faithfully,
John Kenneth Galbraith

Department of State
Washington
June 4, 1963

Mr. President:

I suspect that your observations on women[36] are right although doubtless there is something involving some fairly fundamental (and interesting) relations with men which leads to an absence of independent and tough durability. This is unquestionably more serious in politics than in (say) writing or painting although apart from the nineteenth century it is surprising how few good women writers there have been and fewer artists.

In politics, however, I think of two major exceptions to this rule. One obviously was the first Elizabeth who was obviously a commanding, durable and highly competent operator. She knew that it was bad politics to be bloodthirsty; but she was also devoid of sentiment. The other case, although she was superficially more sentimental, was Mrs. Roosevelt. In American liberal politics (especially domestic matters) she was about as detached and clear headed as anybody I ever knew.

J. Kenneth Galbraith

October 23, 1963

Dear Mr. President:

In response to various messages from Baruch[37] since my return, I called on him last week. He submitted the following moderately encouraging report on your Administration:

(1) You will be considered a fine President.
(2) You are the first in the office in his lifetime—ninety-three years—"with really good manners." The Churchill ceremony made a deep impression on the old boy.
(3) Your best score will be on civil rights.
(4) You have to carry too much of the political load yourself. Your Cabinet lacks political medicine- and hatchet-men of the highest caliber. The Attorney General is fine.
(5) He is opposed to tax reduction but won't say so.

Assuming an endorsement (with underwriting) might be useful next year, I urge something like the attached.

I will have some thoughts for you for Pennsylvania.

Yours faithfully,
John Kenneth Galbraith

Enc.

Dear Mr. Baruch:

Our friend Galbraith has just told me of your talk a few days ago. I am happy to learn that so many of our policies have your approval. On some things—I gather from Galbraith that the tax bill is one—a President is likely to find himself differing at times from even his most respected and experienced advisers. I hope that even in the cases where we disagree, I will continue to have the benefit of your thoughts.

I trust that you continue in the best of health.

Yours sincerely,
John F. Kennedy

1960. Intense discussion at a convention caucus of the farm states. Could someone from Massachusetts give thought to the farms? "Franklin D. Roosevelt was also an easterner." Courtesy of the author.

An American ambassador should always stand out. Joining JKG here at Palam Airport in March of 1962 is Jawaharlal Nehru. Next is Jacqueline Kennedy and then her sister Lee Radziwill. On either side are numerous Indian and American notables. Courtesy of the author.

The White House: an informal meeting comes to an end.
Courtesy of the author.

II

Economics

March 13, 1959

Senator John F. Kennedy
United States Senate Office Building
Washington, D.C.

Dear Jack:

I wonder if I could add a word or two about the paper I left on Wednesday. I think it states the essentials of the problem, but it goes a step farther than I would imagine it politic for you to go in public expression. Your stand on wages and prices on "Meet the Press" just after the elections struck the right tone. After all, it is the function of the economist to stay a little out in front—and also to collect the blows.

Also, while you are safe in attacking the tight money policy, you shouldn't make the attack quite as strong as I do.[1] It has a great many well intentioned defenders.

The statement on fiscal policy is the one I would stand on. We can afford a deficit when there is unemployment, and we should balance the budget when there is full employment. One will always encounter the argument that the Federal Government should conduct its affairs like the average family and balance income and outgo. I have always found the most useful answer to this that the Federal Government, by unbalancing its budget, can help the man who needs a job balance his budget.

Yours faithfully,
J. K. Galbraith

October 20, 1960

Senator John F. Kennedy
United States Senate Office Building
Washington, D.C.

Dear Jack:

There is a current and considerable commotion about gold which may concern you in the next day or so or in the debate.[2] Yesterday there was an unprecedented increase in its price on the London free market—26$\frac{1}{2}$ cents to $35.60 an ounce. The counterpart of this is a weakening of the dollar—i.e., more dollars to buy an equivalent weight of gold. And since the price here remains at $35.00, actually 35.08\frac{3}{4}$, and the shipping and insurance cost is 12 cents, it means that there is pressure to withdraw here at that price to export and sell at the London price. Withdrawals so far this year have been fairly heavy, as you know—through last Wednesday, $842 million.

Quite a dither could develop over this. Thus last night, Karl Brandt, a highly conservative member of the Council of Economic Advisers, sent me word asking that I urge you to issue a statement of reassurance to halt what he called "the panic." I didn't respond. It seemed obvious that if the Administration has something to say, it should be to you directly and officially.

As to your position: I am not sure that any great change is called for although it might perhaps be sharpened up. We should be concerned but not alarmed. But we *must* be very certain that we are not put on the defensive—the Republican strategy will be to say "See how the world mistrusts the Democrats. They are to blame." And we must avoid anything that could be in any degree construed as irresponsible.

To avoid being put on the defensive, we must pin the problem on the Administration—where indeed it belongs. I would say: "This is not a new development. Republican management has been unsatisfactory now for years. It has allowed domestic prices to get out of line; as a result we have priced ourselves out of foreign markets and our own. Our economy has been growing but slowly; we are competing with more vigorous economies which have been adding new and modern plant. There is fear of recession here which adds to the present uncertainty. These shortcomings a Democratic Administration will move promptly to correct. The world will have renewed confidence in the American economy under Democratic guidance.

"A Democratic Administration will also display greater economic fiscal responsibility. We will have a sound and sensible policy on prices and wages. We will plug tax loopholes. We will spend less on agriculture. We will put the health program under Social Security with its own source of revenue. As I have said, repeatedly, my policy is that of a balanced budget save only in severe recession. The Eisenhower Administration, by contrast, had a deficit of $12.5 billions in 1957–58, the largest in peacetime history.[3]

"We will not, as I have also repeated, tinker with the dollar. Nor will we impose restrictions on the export of capital or gold. A healthy stable economy does not need to worry about its gold supply. We shall have that kind of an economy."

An important historical parallel suggests itself here. In 1932 and before inauguration in 1933, there was a large outflow of gold. This was stopped and reversed by Roosevelt. Then as now it was poor economic performance under the Republicans which probably created the uncertainty. Then as now there was an effort to blame it on the forthcoming Democratic Administration. And in both cases conservatives were quick to suggest that the balance of payments problem meant that needed social legislation would have to be postponed. FDR resisted such suggestions. I doubt that you will be more susceptible.

On one point the parallel does not hold. FDR embargoed gold exports and raised the price of gold. That was to restore the domestic price level. There is no occasion for this now. And there must not be *the slightest* suggestion of it. A loose word on this could cause us endless trouble, embarrassment and perhaps many votes.

I am speaking in New York again this week at 40 Central Park South (EL. 5–1346 or EL. 5–0820) and am on call except when occupied with my high-level rabble-rousing.

Yours faithfully,
J. K. Galbraith

November 17, 1960

President-Elect John F. Kennedy
North Ocean Boulevard
Palm Beach, Florida

Dear Jack:

I am half ashamed to add to the free advice you are getting these days but I have been thinking a good deal about the gold and balance-of-payments problem in relation to the Treasury and I venture to pass my thoughts along. I can at least claim disinterest; I must be the only Democrat in the country who isn't yearning for a big desk and leather chairs. (They are even calling me by the dozens on the suspicion that I might be a wheel.)

The choice we face, which is curiously like the one before FDR in 1933, is rather clear: We can try to hold gold here by seeking to inspire confidence while we cut our overseas outlays and try to shift the burden to others. Interest rates will be kept attractive in relation to those abroad and Washington policy will be as somber as possible. Domestic action which might lead to a flight from the dollar will be muted. We will, in a measure, make policy in the light of the fears of the Swiss, Germans and our own financial community.

The alternative is to accept the challenge, and the risks, of a much more aggressive policy. We still have time and reserves that give us some room for maneuver. There is no license to waste money abroad as we do now on dependents, the little Levittowns, and (in my judgment) on some of our troop disposition such as the two divisions in Korea. But the main thing is to get the money. So we drive for more exports; we have a wage and price policy that keeps us competitive abroad and at home; we launch a productivity drive and make up the cost by closing the useless tax loopholes; we use production payments to make our farm products competitive; we drive hard to get access to the Common Market; we move on a Western Hemisphere trading area; and, perhaps most important, we lead strongly on a policy to get concerted action on interest rate and monetary policy among the industrial countries so this is not dictated by the country in which traditional banking attitudes are strongest. A multilateral central banking policy should be one of the first initiatives.

It will not come to you as a breathtaking surprise that I think we should follow the second course nor do I have any doubt as to your view. I would urge, however, that the choice governs the Secretary of the Treasury. The second course will require a very strong and aggressive team in the Treasury and it is worth accepting some chagrin in Wall Street to get it. The latter, indeed, is unavoidable since instinctively or otherwise, it opts for the first course. I do not think one can get vigorous action from the banker-statesman such as McCloy or Dillon[4] which the Establishment is so energetically urging. I would fear that you would be faced with the same sad lack of initiative which, indeed, has brought us to the present situation.

My thoughts on the alternatives run to the intelligent political leaders who have made a record on such matters—Richard Bolling, Albert Gore, possibly Henry Reuss.[5] (Douglas would, I suppose, be ideal.)[6] They should then be backed up by the numerous and effective younger men who are yearning to get their teeth in this problem. With the bankers one won't get these younger men; the excuses for inaction will be reinforced on down the line. But most important, and this is the case for the congressional leaders, the chances for dealing with the unions on wages, getting tax reform and working with agriculture will be seriously circumscribed. And these are essential.

So be it. Could I conclude with a word on another problem. Four years from now, if the farmers remember you are a friend, they will forget you are a Catholic. Then you can outdo 1936.[7] This means a good Secretary of Agriculture and all the more for, while you are going to be your own Secretary of State and probably of Treasury, you can't be a farmer too. It is the worst job in Washington. All the good men will want something else; the idiots will apply by the dozen for that reason.

The need is for someone who is strong and bright and, above all, who—in the manner of Wallace[8] in his prime—can get a clear picture of the problem and keep it. There will be much talk of "acceptability" to various groups. This in agriculture gets you the lowest common denominator short of larceny.

Who fills the bill I am far from sure. My first thought was Freeman[9] who made sense on the subject in the Advisory Council. However, he would have to be enthusiastic for the job which he might not be. Or McGovern[10] whom I do not know. But I think the ideal man is probably Lauren K. Soth. He is Editor of the Des Moines Register-Tribune. He has written well and wisely on the subject (I got Princeton to publish one of his books), is learned and sympathetic, charming, from the right part of the country, and an entirely fresh figure.* His paper supported Dick but he was at least morally for you.

I am sorry to impose all of this on you. Along with the people who like to hear themselves talk, there are, unquestionably, some who are even more inordinately attracted by their own composition. I may well be entitled to a gold star membership in both groups.

Yours faithfully,
J. K. Galbraith

* Also justifiably popular in the Midwest. As to his willingness, I would hope but not guess.   JKG

United States Senate
Washington, D.C.
November 21, 1960

Professor Kenneth Galbraith
Harvard University
Cambridge, Massachusetts

Dear Ken:

Do you think that you can get me up a memorandum on how we could organize and implement your suggestion for a "tri-partite guiding group with well spelled out goals" per your discussion in U.S. News this week.[11] Can it be done by Executive action or by statutory authority?

After we get it in some form we could take it up with Reuther, Dubinsky, McDonald and Meany.[12]

Secondly, do you think that it would be advisable to set up a task force on national tax policy, the report to be ready by the end of December? If so, who should be put on it and who should chair it?

I hope to be talking to you after I get back from my vacation. In the meantime, may I hear from you?

Sincerely,
John F. Kennedy

November 29, 1960

President-Elect John F. Kennedy
3307 N Street, N.W.
Washington, D.C.

Dear Jack:

Your letter of November 21 concerning taxes and organization for price and wage stability showed up only today. The Post Office may be a key spot.

Meantime, Mike Feldman had called me on the tax matter and I had suggested names including Stan Surrey here at the Law School.[13] My only question is whether this should be made an emergency matter. The income tax is badly in need of overhauling in the interests of substantial equity and all tax legislation takes a long time. Since time will be required in any case, perhaps an effort should be made to do the whole job.

I will turn my hand to the wage and price paper just as soon as I have a moment. In any case, I will have it for you by early next week.

Yours faithfully,
J. K. Galbraith

December 5, 1960

President-Elect John F. Kennedy
3307 N Street, N.W.
Washington, D.C.

Dear Jack:

I have an abnormal accumulation of thoughts on dollars, Latin America, casting, agriculture, foreign aid and recessions which I would gladly share with you. Apart from the undoubted nourishment to my ego—nothing, I would gather, is so rampant these days as the desire to be known as a constructive force—perhaps it might be useful.

I am, of course, at your call. And since it is well known that I deal with affluence from a solvent base, Washington or Florida are equally satisfactory.

Yours faithfully,
J. K. Galbraith

December 7, 1960

President-Elect John F. Kennedy
3307 N Street, N.W.
Washington, D.C.

Dear Jack:

You have long astonished me on the things you find time to read, and this might be a relatively painless and balanced view of the dollar problem.[14] My disclaimer as your economic adviser is the standard one. It serves principally to persuade people that my influence is vast.

Yours faithfully,
J. K. Galbraith

Enc. article in *Commercial and Financial Chronicle*

Harvard University
Cambridge, Massachusetts
December 30, 1960

President-Elect John F. Kennedy
North Ocean Boulevard
Palm Beach, Florida

Dear Mr. President:

I was in St. Louis this week and on Wednesday, in line with our Palm Beach chat, I flew up to St. Paul and spent the afternoon with Governor Freeman.[15] He is preparing himself for his new task with great energy and none of the badly concealed repugnance with which most statesmen and all presidential candidates react to all agricultural questions. Here for you, and rather more for your staff, are the main lines of our exchange.

(1) The farm problem is solvable and perhaps without excessive difficulty. The trouble is that no one for years has really tried to solve it—to use the firm controls, cross-compliance, expanded low-income use, production payments and the other elements of any good plan.

(2) This is because, in the present obscene state of farm politics, there is well-entrenched opposition to every single thing that must be done. Action, therefore, will bring screams or simulated screams of pain. These must be expected, and should not be blamed when they come on the "brash young Governor" from Minnesota. In the end, the sound course of politics is to get this mess worked out—and as long before 1964 as possible.

(3) Immediately farmers will react sympathetically to any change from Benson[16] so there will be underlying good will with some effect on Congress. In dealing with the opposition, we should not lose sight of the fact that, the election being as it was, we are singularly free of commitments.

(4) Full use should be made, to the point of criticism, of existing legislative authority. This is large. The new Secretary must assure himself of the most competent legal guidance through this legal morass.

(5) In planning legislation, anything that might look like (and be shot down as) a Freeman Plan must be avoided. Apart from special legislative requirements, such as the removal of the wheat acreage limitation, the legislative strategy is to get broad enabling legislation along the lines of the Humphrey Bill. This should be sought early. Being old legislation, it is not likely to be labelled as "a Plan." A vote against will be a vote for Benson. And defeat would not be absolutely fatal.

(6) Balance-of-payments considerations will support one important change. Briefly, our agriculture, being very efficient, is a prime export possibility. Support prices, however, prop us out of world markets. Production payments would let prices be at world and hence competitive levels. Our own farmers would get their extra payment off the top. In our present situation, to earn foreign currency is more important than to save domestic dollars. Cotton is a

clear case for this technique. So we tie a desirable step in farm legislation to our international needs.

(7) There must be a close watch for hanky-panky in commodity stabilization and storage operations. Things may be all right. But there are rumors.

(8) The U.S.D.A. (provisionally) is top-heavy on the top side which is a Republican tendency. Specifically, the layer of assistant secretaries between the Secretary and the operating divisions of the U.S.D.A. may well, as in the case of the Pentagon, be more of a barrier than a help to a working Secretary. If these assistant secretaries operate, they are in the way; if they don't, they are, in the immortal words of James J. Hill when he compared the railway passenger business to the male nipple, "neither decorative nor useful."

(9) The farm credit agencies and especially the Farmers' Home Administration need prompt rejuvenation and a new view of their responsibilities. They are set up to provide loans to worthy but needy risks. They have come to judge themselves by whether they have a perfect repayment record. To get this, they must loan to the people who don't need help or could get it from the bank. They have done little to relieve the current farm credit stringency.

(10) Before we commit ourselves to a food stamp plan, we should have another look at it. It might be good and it could be a liberal cliche. Certainly we should let our minds dwell on alternatives. For example, why not make a food allotment certificate a natural and perfectly standard supplement to unemployment compensation—a way of increasing it? Use it not for prunes and other surplus items but for meat and milk. Expanded production of these is one of the first ways of making inroads on our food supplies. (It takes some seven acres to nourish a man on meat to the one that will keep him alive if he eats cereals.) Also couldn't nutrition be tied in affirmatively to the fitness program? No youngster should do physical exercise (or play touch football) on an empty stomach.

(11) It may be that the right farm program, especially with production payments, won't save much money. We will probably get more durable applause for a solution than for economy.

> Yours faithfully,
> J. K. Galbraith

cc: Mr. Sorensen

Memorandum for the President
From: John Kenneth Galbraith
Subject: The Recession and What Now

Two or three weeks ago you asked me for a final memorandum on economic policy. This I happily submit.

The Prospect

Although the Administration has produced a spate of predictions of an upturn in the last two or three weeks, the truth is that no one including the predictors knows what is going to happen. We do know that present economic performance is unsatisfactory, that things are not yet getting better very fast and there is further and important agreement that even a good showing will leave us with a high level of unemployment for many months to come. These are the only hard facts (as distinct from the predictions) on which we can make policy.

The Choices

As the time for the promised April review approaches, three courses of action are open. They are:

(1) Wait a while longer
(2) Cut taxes
(3) Do something better

As to the first, we should not appear over-eager and apologetic about what we are doing or too inclined to dash on to something new. And little of the legislation we have requested has been enacted. Still the economic situation will be no more favorable—production will be no higher and unemployment no lower—than when we promised the review at the beginning of February. On balance it might be a bit worse. So action is in order if there is anything wise and needful to do.

I am against a tax cut. I was most reluctant about urging it on Ike in 1958; my feelings have not changed. It is the kind of experimental step which the Congress will debate for a long while so its practical effect will not be quick. And it stretches our education in modern economics to the limit to cut taxes while we increase our spending.

But there are more fundamental objections. Once we start talking about tax cuts we will take pressure off the rest of your program as a prop to the economy. We now say that housing, school building and urban renewal are needed both for themselves and for their effect on employment. Given the tax cut conservatives will not be slow to say that this will do the job. Finally, too much about tax reduction has to be explained. The unemployed man has to be told that we cannot much increase his benefits but we can reduce the taxes on the stiff who has a job. We will have to explain—indeed I will have to explain—to the underdeveloped lands why we can afford only fairly modest aid programs at a time when we are cutting taxes at home. Our upper middlebrow critics will note that the Democrats after complaining about the relative inadequacy of public investment have now proceeded to increase private consumption. The case for tax reduction in short is based on a preliminary and partial view of our situation. I deeply respect those who argue for it; I am only sorry that in this instance they are wrong.

Procedure

The alternatives fall into two parts. The first step is to reverse effectively the tight money policy which most economists agree precipitated the recession* and which today, eight months after the depression began, still gives us rates of interest almost as high as at its beginning. These interest rates simply must not continue. The justification for the high rates—the "prime" or anchor rate of the big New York banks, the still astronomic mortgage rates charged to the depressed building industry on down to the high rates on government issues—could not be clearer. It is not to prevent inflation; the economy is in a state of deflation and expansion is what we seek. It is not to hold gold; that situation is stable. In fact these rates have the same fundamental function as high prices: they are for those who get them. They keep up the revenues of those with money to lend.

The Treasury or at least Secretary Roosa[17] agrees on the need for a further cut. Our only difference is one of magnitude and urgency.

The Federal Reserve is totally discouraging. It could help without adding to your budget concerns—as it did help Eisenhower. It talks of "nudging"—nudging for God's sake—down the long-term rate, and there have been hints that this might stop in view of the likelihood of recovery. Chairman Martin[18] has expressed doubts about whether the long-term rate can be much reduced. No similar doubts have ever been expressed about the feasibility of raising—witness the breakneck speed with which rates were raised after 1958. What is much more striking, while the Federal Reserve has repeatedly emphasized the need for restraint and its fear of inflation it has rarely expressed any comparable concern for expanding output and increasing employment. Independence has become the design for maintaining the affiliation with those who lend money as distinct from people who need jobs. This is the unpleasant but unadorned truth.

The second part of the strategy is to intervene with more money where it will be prompt in effect, help those who need the help most and, out of respect for your fiscal sensibilities, not be a burden on the permanent budget. This also I think can be done.

Specific Action

Here are the needed measures under the two heads:

Part I. *Monetary Policy.* My recommendations on this are set forth in the attached letter.[19] It is based on my feeling that pressure will get results. Central banks have long been in conflict with the executive power, the latter reflecting popular need. When the issue is joined the banks never win or put up much of a fight. I must stress that I am not looking for a fight but only that we have a vital issue to be faced.

Part II. *Fiscal Policy.* If I interpret your budget policy correctly, it has been to get rid, once and for all, of the allegation that we are reckless spenders. At the same time it seeks to do what must be done. This policy clearly excludes a general lifting of spending sights. But I would like to argue that it does not exclude a policy of keeping the present budget limitations and launching supplementary assistance to those who are out of work. This latter, if confined to the unemployed, is temporary for it will be discontinued with reemployment. And unlike either tax reduction or general spending it puts the help where it is most needed. I would like to argue for a special omnibus bill—The Special Assistance Act of 1961 it might be called—with the following components:

(1) A supplementary assistance program for families of unemployed based on the number of children. This is now available on a relief basis. It would be extended to all unemployed and public assistance families at the rate of so much per child per month. It would be hard to vote against this help and it would be a great source of comfort and kindness to the unemployed families. It would end automatically when the wage earner gets a job. And heads of families are not likely to malinger.

(2) Emergency grants and loans for public facilities in towns with serious unemployment so long as unemployment exceeds a given percentage. The community uses its unemployed to fix itself up. When unemployment declines, eligibility lapses.

(3) A system of combined grants and/or deferred interest-bearing loans to unemployed families to buy materials and paint to fix up or improve their houses. This is a highly plausible use of the unemployed man's time. It could be designed, I think, to apply to rental housing as well. Again when unemployment drops the demand for these loans disappears.

(4) A Youth Conservation Corps to catch the unemployed teen agers. This alone of the measures might be part of the permanent budget.

So be it. Should the foregoing be unacceptable there is still clean living and regular prayer.

* Arthur F. Burns, economist extraordinary to Eisenhower, said "the advance of long-term interest rates after mid-1958 was faster than in a comparable stage of any business-cycle expansion during the past century."

Memorandum for the President
From: John Kenneth Galbraith
Subject: Economic Policy[20]

I welcome the opportunity to offer a few conclusions on the state of the domestic economy. These are for such general circulation as you deem desirable. I think I currently detect differences of views within the Administration on matters where, in fact, a clear view of the problem would lead to a strongly unified position. Let me make the following points:

(1) The fiscal policy of the Administration—its spending and taxation—are now set until next January, emergency action in the field of national security apart. This part of the book being closed there is no point in arguing about it except in the unlikely event of a shortage of other subjects for controversy.

(2) Unemployment remains very high. This is in spite of the very large number of people currently employed in foretelling the economic future. In fact no one knows for sure the rate and durability of economic recovery. So long as it exists the large amount of involuntary idleness must be the central concern of our economic policy.

(3) While unemployment has been high, prices have been stable. Hence, except in some purely hypothetical sense, it is unemployment and not inflation about which we must worry. Unemployment is the clear, present and prospective danger.

(4) The talk of inflation comes in part from one of the more remarkable, pervasive and effective influences in American life, namely the New York advocates of higher interest. This community is able to develop a case for higher rates to fit any eventuality and does. Four months ago rates needed to be high to protect our gold stocks. Now they must be high to prevent inflation. If prices were to fall next month they would have to be high as a purely precautionary measure. To my knowledge lower rates have never been urged. Nor is it ever suggested that high rates are good for people or institutions with money to lend. No other high price is defended with such sanctimony. However, the phenomenal level of bank earnings in recent times suggests that, accidentally or otherwise, the high price of money does pay off.

(5) Should inflation become a threat in the next year, the active force shoving up prices will be wage contracts that force up prices with the latter leading, in turn, to further pressure on wages. Higher interest rates make no contact with this cause of inflation. The only hope is by direct negotiation through Secretary Goldberg's new machinery.

(6) It would be reasonable to ask for wage stabilization as part of a package which also provides high employment. We cannot ask the unions to take unemployment and wage stabilization too. Thus, even an effective attack on the wage-price spiral, the immediate source of inflation, must be combined with an effective attack on unemployment.

(7) The fiscal policy being set for the next several months and unemployment being high, the only available action against unemployment is low interest rates leading to easy borrowing conditions and a high rate of investment. This policy is an imperative. To tighten interest rates now is the exact reverse of wisdom.

(8) The longer run political effects of such a high premature tight money policy would be especially unfortunate for the institutions associated with it. Unemployment at its present levels, it will be agreed by all, is politically and socially indefensible. Yet, if the Federal Reserve should urge or the Treasury acquiesce in rising interest rates they will be defending the indefensible. There is no chance that their role will be unnoticed. I venture to urge that the Federal Reserve, especially, cannot afford to be known for very long as the sponsor of unemployment.

(9) I come now to action. The first step is to be clear that the continuing problem is unemployment. Federal Reserve action and statements should, in particular, be clearly premised on this fact.

(10) Purchases in the long-term market should continue and on an effective scale. As an earnest of unity and seriousness of purpose, given the present levels of idleness, the rediscount rate should be moderately reduced. This would be a step of the most salutary importance. The explanation should stress the high level of unemployment and idle capacity.

(11) These steps would give an unequivocal aspect to Federal Reserve Policy and this is important. The objective is to reduce the retail and mortgage rates—the rates that effectively influence investment, employment and the rate of growth. Given the pressure for

higher money prices these rates will only fall if there is clear indication that this is the direction of policy.

(12) I conclude with one more general point. A sensible monetary policy is our *only* available instrument against unemployment in the next few months. Given the attractiveness of higher interest rates to those who receive them and the genuine admiration for this policy by those it benefits, we cannot escape attack if we press for lower rates. We should be braced for it and weigh it against the criticism we will have from our friends and the jeers we shall have from our enemies if unemployment remains at present or anywhere near present levels.

Moreover, in the larger world arena it is surely better that we have criticism from the bankers for low interest rates than from the workers for no jobs. There is sometimes a temptation in moments of crisis to argue for a conservative domestic policy. In the present crisis we must have a domestic policy that proves that our system works. Pre-eminently that means that it provide jobs.

New Delhi, India
April 17, 1962

Dear Mr. President:

I am sure you have heard from everyone on the steel operation, but I think I might claim a special word.[21] For my right to take satisfaction is, in some sense, that of the spiritual father of the policy. I was, I imagine, the first fairly respectable economist to argue for inflation control by exercising a vigorous and firm role in the industrial price and wage making and to hold that the need for this is a deeply organic fact of modern industrial organization.

I wonder, in this connection, if your mind goes back to a discussion at Arthur's house just after your re-election in 1958. You were going on "Meet the Press" the following night. We talked of this issue and you carried forward the thread of discussion into the first plain argument for bringing the public interest to bear on the wage-price bargain by any major American political leader. I listened with more enthusiasm than you would have guessed. Now, a mere four years later, the policy is firmly established and indeed has been carried into effect for the most important product and in face of a classical manifestation of resistance. With the primacy of the public interest affirmed in this way it is now possible to allow demand to expand much more liberally without danger of inflation. As a result, we can come far closer to full employment. It means, incidentally, that our economic policy comes abreast of the best of European design.

Well, you will see that for once I am without complaint. The whole operation, incidentally, is a marvelous example of Kennedy political technique. Roosevelt would not have done it nearly as well. He would have aroused fervent support on his side, but in one way or another, he would have forced a great many people to align themselves on the other. The Corporation would have taken comfort in this support and kept up the price. Your technique of allowing the bastards to isolate themselves and then striking with real fury was an infinitely more artistic operation.

I have, incidentally, a local reaction to the episode. Though with some misgivings, I had agreed to a major role for the Steel Corporation in the planning of the new steel plant here. And the Indians had reluctantly agreed. The Corporation had then responded with the demand that the smaller steel firms be excluded. The local press gave a major play to what it moderately described as the Corporation's arrogance and double-cross. I am afraid if we go ahead with the Corporation we will spend our money and get credit for only shoehorning a highly obdurate firm into the local scene.

> Yours faithfully,
> John Kenneth Galbraith

Newfane, Vermont
May 29, 1962
(dictated by telephone)

Memorandum for the President
Subject: The Stock Market

The stock market slump is of consequence, and I venture some suggestions.[22]

(1) The cause of the drop is that people have ceased to see an

unlimited prospect for capital gains. This is partly out of respect for the Administration anti-inflation measures. That means that common stocks will not rise forever for reasons of inflation. And as the inflation danger lessens, so does the demand for stock as an inflation hedge. However, as always, speculation has vastly exaggerated this movement. The great reality is that you can make money out of the market when it is going up if you sell when it starts going down. Lots of people have been making money. They are now trying to sell. Yesterday's movement was one of the inevitable results.

(2) The argument as to whether stock movements foretell economic movements is a footless one. As you said rightly the other day, sometimes they do and sometimes they don't. But there is no question that a bad crack-up in the market can have serious repercussions on the economy. Although it was considered highly uncouth to say so—and almost no one did—the 1929 crash was a major factor in the collapse in the economy that followed. Investment decisions are sensitive to the market. Also people spend capital gains and are influenced in their spending by what is happening to capital gains. There was a readily traceable effect from the market to other middle-class spending in 1929 and the impact on all consumer spending was quantitatively considerable.

(3) Similar effects also significant in their effect must be expected as a result of recent market behavior. These will have a depressing effect on investment and on consumer spending. I would expect housing, real estate investment, automobiles, home furnishings to be especially affected.

(4) The Administration should adhere to the following rules in the present situation:

(a) keep down the number of reassuring statements. Everyone will be tempted to rush in with magic words to calm the fever. The words will quickly be discounted to zero, or—as in the case of Mr. Hoover—to something less. Very soon everyone looks foolish.

(b) hold rigidly to the explanation that the market is accommodating itself to the end of inflation, the diminished prospect for capital gain, and the speculative disappointment associated with the latter. Say that for these reasons the termination of inflation was bound to bring a sharp readjustment. This explanation has the advantage of being valid; of separating the issue of inflation from that of employment, profit and production levels, and minimizing uneasiness about the latter; and it is the explanation most conducive to confidence in the dollar abroad.

(c) at the same time, everyone must recognize that the effect of the stock market drop will be depressing on the economy. Accordingly all forms of budget liberalization and any needed steps to keep money rates easy and encourage investment are of increased urgency. As usual, I would be against a tax cut.

I am sending you a copy of my history of the 1929 episode which, by the kind of foresight that can only inspire confidence, has just become available in a new and inexpensive edition.[23]

J. K. Galbraith

May 31, 1962

Memorandum for the President
Subject: The Gold Flow Again

As you know the briefest sojourn in this Republic turns my thoughts back to this ineluctable topic. However this is not another diagnosis but a checklist of things, some of them rather off the beaten track, which ought to be considered. I am sensitive to the likelihood that, without my knowledge, several are getting attention.

Let me note that every measure which affects the situation in an important way looks difficult. That is because there are strong vested interests, pecuniary and ideological, in things as they are and in the outflow itself. Every conceivable action will thus be in conflict with one of these vested positions—with the liberal view of trade and aid, the Rockefeller Brothers *cum* Establishment view of troop deployment, and anti-communist strategy, the businessman's preferences on taxation and investment, the rich man's preferences for the Costa Brava and the serviceman's preferences on connubiality and love. Exponents of trade liberalization will be especially aroused by some of these suggestions—for them trade liberalization is not a policy but an altar. Some remedies can be ruled out because they are not useful or not worth the trouble. None can be ruled out in principle or because it is troublesome. I begin with ritualistic mention of three useful courses which need not be explored.

(1) Devaluation. I still hear misguided talk about this—it is as irresistible to some economists as alcohol to the Iroquois. Sterling, Canadian dollars, roubles and pesos can all be devalued but the dollar cannot. It is the standard against which the others are measured. Should the standard change they will change to keep their accustomed position. Nothing important would be changed and the loss of confidence in the process would be frightful.

(2) Accommodation of our policy to holders of overseas claims. This means doing what the Swiss bankers would wish us to do. They are, on the whole, egotistical reactionaries who will prescribe in accordance with their always myopic and often medieval instincts. The ear of the United States cannot be so bent.

(3) Follow a more conservative monetary and fiscal policy. This is related. It was necessary to get control of internal inflation to protect the dollar. But the vital step, subjecting the wage-price spiral to effective restraint, has now been accomplished. If the price line can be held there is no need to sacrifice domestic production and employment. Nor is it clear that a non-expansionist policy would protect the dollar. France, Germany and Italy have obviously been combining vigorous domestic with vigorous export expansion.

I come now to affirmative steps. Some affect the basic balance. Some have only to do with where assets of Americans are held and thus affect gold movements but not the fundamental asset position. All proceed from the valid view that our present earnings in foreign commerce are not sufficient to sustain our foreign outlays plus the investment flow and that, while operating on all dimensions of the problem, we must stress those which will get fairly prompt results. I put proposals in the form of questions.

(1) Why not create a presumption in favor of American products and travel?

During the dollar shortage years Americans were told that they helped the world when they bought imported goods. This of course is no longer true. During this year to date imports have been rising rapidly in relation to exports. Without launching a Buy American campaign the government should make it clear that where price and quality are comparable it helps to buy at home. I would suggest a press conference question and answer to this effect. It should come into Administration speeches. The pundits will catch the drift and should be quietly encouraged to do so. If done carefully there will be nothing that will invite retaliation. In any case other countries do it as a matter of course. It is always patriotic to buy a British car. The American people are very responsive to similar patriotic suggestions. The effect is largely confined to manufactured consumer's goods.

(2) Can we reduce indirect leakages in the aid program?

In addition to the aid they receive aided countries have earnings from merchandise trade with the United States. To a considerable extent our aid frees the earned dollars for use elsewhere. India, for example, sells about a quarter billion worth of jute, tea, cashews, textiles and travel to the United States and uses around a $100 million to cover its huge balance of payments deficit with the West Germans. (These figures are from memory.) I should be instructed to tell the Indians that continuation of aid necessarily depends on their guiding a much larger part of their dollar earnings back to the United States. Similar pressure should be put on similarly situated governments. This would press home to the Germans (and others) the need for financing their own exports rather than relying on us for the money.

(3) Should the flow of private investment be controlled?

I am reluctantly inclined to think that the time has come when sizable exports of capital—chunks exceeding say $5,000,000—and going to Western Europe should be brought within the purview of the government. Can powers be found that would allow of this by executive action?

(4) Should we encourage the repatriation of runaway wealth?

The United States carries large burdens in the world at large risk. Quite a few American citizens have sought to contract out of cost and risk by keeping their assets abroad. That is their privilege but one they can reasonably be asked to pay for. Americans living here or abroad should be asked to register overseas holdings in excess of (say) a quarter million dollars. These external holdings should then be subject to a modest wealth tax. Both registration and tax would lead to repatriation and the prospect would discourage further flight. There would be some evasion but at this income level people do not like to be outside the law.

(5) Should we discourage long-term residence abroad?

American refugees from the rigors of American taxes, living costs and servantless existence have become a prominent feature of every European city and resort. At a time when we are worrying about the spending of dependents of soldiers we can hardly ignore the expenditures of millionaires in Gstaad and Antibes. Perhaps there might be a special non-resident passport for those who are not vocationally required to reside abroad. Renewal would get progressively more expensive—after a year $500. After five years $1,000. Obviously this is meant only to be suggestive. But it would set the signals against long-term residence abroad which is important.

(6) Are we looking seriously at troop deployment in relation to dollar costs?

Our present deployment is based on tradition, accident, the mystique of the conventional force, and the recurrent feeling that, in the absence of any other feasible lines of action, the movement of troops might help. (I hasten to allow for rational factors as well.) On the whole dollars have not entered the calculation at least until lately. It is much better that they enter as a consideration now than on some subsequent day when we run out. At least why not have a high-powered team draw up a deployment strategy designed to minimize the dollar outlay. The logistical framework and small forces would remain forward. Behind our dollar account would be the troops (and their families) with great emphasis on mobility and air-lift. We might, as compared for example with the sterile commitment in Korea, find it a lot better.

(7) Have we recently reviewed the cost of our political prebendaries?

Formosa and Korea come to mind. Granted that aid is indispensable—are we providing it in the most economical way? Or is it going in indirectly by way of excessively expensive military establishments? We should remind ourselves that our commitments here were established when dollars were plentiful. A dollar shortage would have been good for Mr. Dulles.

(8) Are we facing fully the fact that in important parts of the world reform is far more urgent and also much cheaper than aid?

In South America it is land reform, above all, that people want. Those who own the land have already been paid for it a thousand times. In the absence of reform our aid does not help the people or even much postpone revolution. Rather it buys the way temporarily around crisis in the process of which dollars are funneled into Rio and squirreled out to Paris. I am aware of the difficulties here and the ease with which one can counsel perfection. But I also gravely suspect the legitimist tendencies of the Department of State. In any case we must someday ring the bell on the big, unpremeditated loans to Latin American governments which do no good and buy only a few weeks time for governments that are as likely to be replaced by better ones as worse.

(9) You already know my feeling on Britain and the EEC. It will be much better for our balance of payments if Britain stays out. The arguments for European unity were once good. It is only that, for us, the age of chivalry is past. I am also sure that it is better for us politically, for our alliance with the British is one of the few substantial and workable liaisons in the world and it will be lost if the British get roped in on the continent. I realize that we can't reverse ourselves now. I would hope that we might not shove unnecessarily and could rejoice modestly if the British do not make it.

J. K. Galbraith

New Delhi, India
July 10, 1962[24]

CONFIDENTIAL

Dear Mr. President:

I read with a good deal of concern about the pressure that is mounting on taxes.[25] I also sense that your instinct is to resist and I hope you continue to do so. I submit the following thoughts:

(1) A very large part of American conservative and business opinion is simply against taxes regardless. It will thus argue with great enthusiasm for tax reduction, quite apart from the consequences fiscal and otherwise about which they couldn't care less. Of course, after the taxes are reduced, these people will not hesitate to attack you for an unbalanced budget. Some of them may be sophisticated enough to hope the new lower tax revenues will set a new lower ceiling on spending. The rest welcome the liberal initiative as assistance from an unexpected quarter.

(2) The momentary alliance with my friends is more apparent than real. The people who are simply anti-tax will want an across-

the-board and upper brackets reduction including, though less urgently, the corporation tax. The liberals and unions will want relief in the withholding brackets and here, of course, it would have its effect on spending. (The effect of upper bracket and corporation tax on business outlays and spending will be slight or negligible.) So a proposal to reduce taxes, while it looks simple and fast, will produce a nasty Congressional brawl with a disagreeable aftermath. What will satisfy the liberals will outrage the rich and vice-versa. Both, in the end, will be angry at the Administration.

(3) From this distance I don't see that the condition of the economy is all that bad. Personal income seems to be holding up very well. The investment plans seem not to have been seriously revised. The stock market is steadier for the moment at a safer level. Unemployment is, to be sure, substantial. But without excusing it, it remains that we have been living with something like this volume of unemployment for a long while. Once we would have thought it creditably low.

(4) Most of what I read on the politics of this situation makes no sense at all. While you are aware of my reluctance to lecture you on this curious subject, perhaps I could make three points: (a) No tax cut has the slightest chance of having the slightest effect on the economy by November. (b) The unemployed are (to their misfortune) a small minority and few can be so silly as to suppose they will do better under the Republicans. (c) The unemployed stiff may have become extremely well educated in recent months but I still can't imagine him applauding the Kennedy Administration for helping him by reducing the taxes of the guy who has a job or the fellow he would be working for if he had a job.

(5) I needn't remind you (but nevertheless I always deem it wise) that the glories of the Kennedy Era will be written not in the rate of economic growth or even in the level of unemployment. Nor, I venture, is this where its political rewards lie. Its glory and reward will be from the way it tackles the infinity of problems that beset a growing population and an increasingly complex society in an increasingly competitive world. To do this well costs the money that the tax reducers would deny.

If the economic outlook for next year is not good, this means that economists and planners should now get down to work on how men can be employed if jobs are needed. Then when next year comes there will be no reason to say that spending for the things that society so desperately needs is too time-consuming a remedy.

With this, I turn my thoughts back to the local scene.

Yours faithfully,
John Kenneth Galbraith

New Delhi, India
August 20, 1962

Dear Mr. President:

I thought your economics lecture[26] very good—in any case I liked the ending. Russ[27] will be proud and you gave the tax-cutters enough support to qualify as the most Keynesian head of state in history. Do put a picture of the Master in your bathroom or some other suitably secluded place. As a charter member of the worshipful following this should give me more pleasure than it does. For, alas, I am left with the thought that the orthodoxy is as always one step behind the problem. And so it is now that Keynes is official.

In an early two-volume work I intend to deal with the relation of a President to economists. I will naturally urge that he listen to them attentively, and indeed with a certain respect and awe. But I will also urge that the political winds in the willows are a safer guide to final action than the most enlightened conclusions of my craft. That is because the President (after all he got elected) must have a sense of what the people want. This is the best guide to action. Economists only know what they should want or, sometimes, what they used to want.

A case in point is economic growth. This is extremely important to economists and about two thousand other people in all the land. This enlightened minority knows that growth is really important. The rest can't remember whether the growth rate is three percent, six percent or ten percent. And instinct tells them that the expanding element in Gross National Product doesn't include the really vital things like food, clothing or fornication which are already excessively available. Nor does it include medical care, schools, or unemployment compensation which they do want but which they know requires some legislation by what Billy Graham once called the Christ-bitten[28] Congress. I couldn't help noticing that immediately after you got through with the charts you got down to child, medical and unemployment care. That is the old political instinct at work. With the principal exception of housing, growth adds the least essential (and the most superfluous) privately-produced goods since we naturally provide ourselves with the most important things first. Needless to say, the addition of more and better depilatories has nothing to do with national health and vigor.

I am also extremely suspicious of official attitudes on the tax burden, so-called. The Gallup poll shows that most people aren't very anxious for a reduction in Federal taxes, a finding which, on past form, you probably noted with some care. The learned view, I am sure, is that people are insufficiently educated in the Keynesian virtues. In their ignorance they groan under the taxes because they fear a deficit and don't want the Government to do anything unsound.

The truth I am sure is that for most people, numerically speaking, the tax take of the Federal Government is not a burden. That is why we can raise so much money in such vast totals with so little complaint. A lot gets picked up in excises or withholding or small quarterly payments that do not really hurt. Others are all too conscious that they didn't do much for the income on which it was levied. Incomes have been increasing. The increased taxes are a fly in an otherwise excellent ointment. If the American people were really suffering under their Federal tax load they would tell Gallup and to hell with the deficit.

Do note that I am talking of Federal taxation. Local taxation is something else again. That is extremely painful, particularly in the new suburbs. Given the ease with which the Federal Government gets money and the difficulty states and localities have in getting theirs, I have long been persuaded that the best kind of tax relief would be generous Federal aid to education.

This bears strongly on the question of tax reform and tax reduction next year. I wonder if it won't be the single most troublesome issue of your Administration. For if I sense matters rightly the only people who do really feel strongly about Federal taxes are the Republican rich who are in the high surtax rates and those who would be were it not for the loopholes. The first will fight for reductions. The second will fight for their loopholes. These two groups will generate the real political steam. Who will be on the other side? Liberals and middle-of-the-roaders won't enter the battle. We are

strongly conditioned to think that it is indecent and a trifle merce-
nary to complain about our taxes, even those on writers. For the
average wage earner and middle class family a reduction though
welcome is not vitally important one way or another. People (as
Adam Smith first observed) are never aroused about a tax they are
accustomed to paying, and we will be reducing taxes to which the
average citizen is thoroughly accustomed. So we shall have the
Republican rich on one side and nobody much on the other. Given
the response of the Congress, we could easily find ourselves with a
remission of taxes for the rich, well-born and Republican and no
other important change.

Yours faithfully,
John Kenneth Galbraith

Harvard University
Cambridge, Massachusetts
September 30, 1963

Dear Mr. President:

Following are some slightly rewarding thoughts in my new role
as a road-company Baruch.[29]

(1) Given our balance-of-payments position, we do not have the
luxury or even the choice of declining a Russian wheat deal.

(2) No one should believe the nonsense about vast Russian gold
reserves. Their behavior has always indicated a great caution in
spending abroad. These purchases mean they must cut back somewhere else. That will be Western Europe at least in part. So we get a
redistribution of reserves in our favor.

(3) The payments balance is weakening our position in Europe
and therewith the Alliance. These sales strengthen our hand. Such
are the uses of adversity when it afflicts the other fellow.

(4) On a new subject. Do have someone write an encouraging letter to Bowles.[30] He is troubled about the downgrading of India and

the Indians and all the other discontents to which ambassadors are subject when they get away from home. I urge this not to keep him happy. He is looking at those memoranda proving how right he was how soon. I am violating a confidence on this so do cover me.

Yours faithfully,
J. K. Galbraith

Harvard University
Cambridge, Massachusetts
October 10, 1963

Dear Mr. President:

I respect as always your mild doubts as to why I should offer political counsel. But I think on the wheat deal,[31] as on the test ban,[32] we have lost momentum by too elaborately meeting the arguments of the opposition. To do so is to suggest that these arguments have merit or more merit than they have.

The wheat deal is a great coup. It could be as politically popular here* as it was in Canada. But it needs a mood of self-confident assertion. "A great opportunity." "Hard to see how anyone could oppose." "Great gain for farmers, taxpayers, balance of payments."

If others are to think it good, we should show no doubts. I urge this mood henceforth, including for food grains.

Yours faithfully,
John Kenneth Galbraith

* In the same quarters, that is.

Harvard University
Cambridge, Massachusetts
November 15, 1963

Dear Mr. President:

As the years pass, you must be growing accustomed to my communiques which, largely in the interests of science, draw attention to my foresight and prescience in economic matters. I am led to favor you with another example in the current case of the balance of payments.

The gain is almost exclusively the result of the drastic interruption of long-term capital outflows. This I take to be confirmation of my contention a) that the control of long-term capital movements is basic to the strategy for the control of the balance of payments and b) that the problem is one that will yield more readily than we suppose to energetic action.

Such firmness is a small political price to pay for the economic gains at home and the political gains abroad that a stronger balance of payments provides. It represents also a considerable moral gain over the ass-kissing of the French central bankers and the Swiss private bankers that is otherwise required. Someone once said that too many people come to love the bonds by which they are tied.

I note finally, and without the slightest suggestion of superior wisdom, that the real gains are all the result of action—the barring of capital exports by a retroactive tax levy—which the Treasury has hitherto excoriated as exchange control. It proves that, willy nilly, we must keep control of these capital outflows.

Yours faithfully,
John Kenneth Galbraith

In India with Jacqueline Kennedy.
Courtesy of the Kennedy Library.

A welcome for Jawaharlal Nehru in Washington. To Kennedy's left are
B. K. Nehru, Indian ambassador to the United States, Secretary of State
Dean Rusk, Vice President Lyndon Johnson, and Prime Minister Nehru.
The two to my left are lost to memory. Courtesy of the Kennedy Library.

With JFK and Nehru in front of the great palaces at Newport, Rhode
Island. Kennedy told Nehru he wanted him to see how the average
American lived. Courtesy of Corbis-Bettmann.

III

Foreign Affairs

United States Senate
Washington, D.C.
January 21, 1959

Professor J. K. Galbraith
Harvard University
Cambridge, Massachusetts

Dear Ken:

It was a happy surprise on my return to Washington to find yet another Galbraith travelogue. Without doubt you have established yourself as the Phineas Fogg of the academic world, and I rather suspect that in the year of 1958 you ran a very good second to John Foster Dulles in international mileage. However, your impressions are indisputably more helpful than the rather turgid commentary which we have been hearing in the Foreign Relations Committee these past days from the Secretary of State and his associates.[1]

As you know I am a member of the Latin America Sub-Committee and I could conceive of nothing better to whet the appetite than these pages. I understand that you also were engaged in some egghead diplomacy on Rhodes this fall. Can we expect a homeric epic on your Aegean travels as well?

With every good wish,

Sincerely,
John F. Kennedy

United States Senate
Washington, D.C.
November 18, 1960

John Kenneth Galbraith
Harvard University
Cambridge, Massachusetts

Dear Ken:

I appreciate very much your recent note.

I plan to be leaving here in about ten days and will be coming to Washington. I would like very much to have a chance to see you. I have a proposal to put to you, which I hope very much you will accept.[2]

Palm Beach is more of the old frontier rather than the new, but it has been very pleasant.

With kind personal regards.

Sincerely,
John F. Kennedy

The White House
Washington
March 22, 1961

Memorandum for: The President
The Secretary of State
From: John Kenneth Galbraith
Subject: Fire Brigade Operations Abroad

I have been reflecting on a problem suggested by recent developments in Bolivia, Iran, Korea and prospectively in Jordan, Viet Nam and elsewhere. This is the case of the country with a disintegrating economy which is the cause and consequence of a disintegrating government. The pattern is familiar. The budget is unbalanced, inflation is endemic. Stabilization efforts are creating industrial and social unrest—or would. American aid, though considerable, is insufficient—perhaps partially as a result of egregious misuse. Maladministration and corruption are general. Underneath is a nauseous social situation in which the landlords and politicians rape the poor with an energy which they apply to no other purpose. Without going into detail, I believe that foreign policy of the recent past including that on aid was peculiarly designed to nurture such developments.

We have also a certain uniformity in reaction when the position becomes dangerous. We send a high level mission. This is done partly because no one can think of anything else to do. But it also makes a measure of sense. It puts the immediate prestige of the United States behind essential social and economic reforms. It enables us to change past policy with grace. And the mission legitimizes the infusion of needed dollars hopefully with safeguards to insure less larcenous employment.

Since the situation is recurrent and widespread, and the remedy is much the same, I am persuaded that these operations should be arranged more thoughtfully than in the past. In the past, each has been an individual crisis: as in the case of the recent mission to Bolivia, an *ad hoc* group was hastily recruited and dispatched.

This is a sloppy and more than slightly dangerous procedure. We have here a rather intricate problem in economic and political diagnosis and therapy. Highly qualified economic knowledge is required of a very rare sort. There is no certainty that sufficiently talented and experienced people of requisite prestige can be assembled on short notice and there is a real chance that the wrong leader will do damage. It would be dubious policy for the Massachusetts General[3] to recruit brain surgeons on a crisis basis whenever someone was brought in with a bad concussion.

Timing is also important. There are instances when conditions must get very bad before corrective action can be taken. But were this combination of economic and political therapy put on a more regular basis preventative action might more often be possible. Thus I am of the impression, based on intelligence from economists working there, that high level pressure on the Iranian government at the moment would avoid a larger outlay of money and a greater likelihood of disorder later on.

Accordingly, I suggest that there be planning for these crises operations since, in fact, they will continue to be a normal aspect of our foreign policy. For the sake of being specific, I suggest that the President and the Secretary of State empanel a small group of men who would be properly qualified and permanently on call for emergency economic and political work abroad. The greatest consideration should be given to their selection for this is work of great subtlety and importance. Members should, with possible exceptions, be men already in government. Their designation should not be publicized but the likelihood of such employment should be known to them. It should be recognized as an assignment of high distinction to take precedence on occasions of need over most regular activity. Some senior official, either in the Department of State or the White House, should be designated to keep in touch with the group. The members should be asked, within reason, to keep themselves informed on situations of potential concern and should have access to relevant cables and dispatches. They should, on occasion, be invited by the Secretary of State to meet for a review of situations of potential concern. Perhaps the group might be accorded some general designation such as "The President's Council on Economic and Political Policy." Such men as Willard Wirtz of the Department of Labor, James Tobin of the Council of Economic Advisers, Edwin Martin of the Department of State, Arthur Schlesinger and Walt Rostow of the White House come to mind as combining the requisite economic and political sophistication but I cite them only by way of example.

The White House
Washington
April 3, 1961

Dear Mr. President:

Could I have your attention for this at, say, your slow 600-word a minute rate?

As I take off I have one concern but a grave one.[4] It grows out of discussions of these last months and my briefing of these past weeks. It is the surviving adventurism in the Administration—an adventurism which counts (or assumes) the gains of some particular operation or enterprise or coup but does not count the larger costs either of success or failure. Our modern history is so replete with disaster of this sort that I am astonished and depressed that the lessons have yet to be fully learned.

The futile campaign to the Yalu ruined the Democrats in 1950.[5] Dulles got Guatemala at the price of losing all South America.[6] The U-2 did not weigh the political cost of failure, especially at that time.[7] We Democrats with our reputation for belligerence and our basically hostile press have far less margin for mistakes than had the Republicans.

The reputation you have already won for your conservative, thoughtful, non-belligerent stance is one of your greatest achievements of these last months. It is also the asset that could be most easily dissipated. I urge you to protect it with all power. This will be my inclination from India, not because I have fallen under the influence of Nehru,[8] am unimaginative or unconcerned about the

Communists but because I think it the prime course of wisdom. I urge as a policy the same restraint, especially when the gains are uncertain, the risks considerable or the executive effects of failure are operating in the Caribbean, elsewhere in Latin America and in Africa.

Respectfully yours,
John Kenneth Galbraith

My affectionate best—as I leave.
JKG

ITS-1[9]

Dear Mr. President:

As I once told you, I think, I propose to revive the ancient and admirable custom of an occasional letter from the envoy if not to his sovereign at least to his sovereign source of authority.[10] Since, however, this practice could easily bitch up modern procedure (to borrow from the stately language of Metternich) I will avoid matters where I am in need of advice or action. These I will put in channels or, in high-level emergency, in a special letter. The present communications, which I propose to label ITS letters—ITS stands for Indo-Talleyrand[11] Series—will be modestly informative and conceivably entertaining and you can read them (or not read them) in the secure knowledge that you will neither encounter (or miss) any crisis. If I have anything in mind it will be simply to let you see something of India and Asia and of its leaders and its problems through the eyes of your ambassador.

We have been here now for a week. I have lunched or dined with all of my senior officers, had lengthy sessions on the various embassy enterprises—politics, economics, aid, USIS, labor, science and other—spoken to the staff, seen Nehru for a lengthy talk, called on the senior Foreign Office officials and encountered a few of my Indian friends. Some of this is legally a bit premature for I do not present my credentials for another day or two.

We were, of course, given an amiable welcome and the radio carried in full my remarks on arrival which, faithful to the fraud of modern communications, I recorded in Beirut and never gave at all. Some fifteen or twenty pounds of garlands were laid on in a manner that must have rejoiced the local florists. Our physical arrangements are enchanting. The residence, a one-time bungalow of the British raj, is small—only three bedrooms—and the principal wall decorations are some large gilt mirrors left behind possibly by Lord Curzon. Some of the furniture was discarded from the White House by Mrs. Warren G. Harding. But basically it is a charming house with a large loggia and a reach of thick green lawn, floral borders in violent color and great trees that are a constant delight. The staff is of alarming size but considerable competence and the cook, while in no danger of being stolen by you, is anxious to please. Your new man may be better on sauces but cannot touch mine in reproducing the Taj Mahal in macaroons. The new Ed Stone Chancery is even more of a delight. Some complain that it is highly unfunctional— water fountains, water gardens and even a few ducks but no office space. You certainly can't please everyone.

The new chancery is located in an uninviting stretch of terrain on the edge of town which has been set aside for embassies. It is flat, dusty and barren. The junior Americans and their Indian staff live in adjacent quarters with slight protection from sun, dust and heat. At this time of the year it is around 90 at midday but before long it will get warm. The Russian embassy and quarters are on one side; on the other side are the British. In both compounds the youngsters splash happily in swimming pools; one was once contemplated for ours but abandoned lest it seem un-American. I have asked for the development of plans. Most of the cost, I might add, will be paid for out of the abundant PL 480 counterpart so that your budget will suffer no more than from a very minor Nubian temple.[12]

The size of the total staff—300 Americans, 726 Indians—came to me as rather a shock. My preliminary impression is of well-mannered, competent and hard-working people of good morale. From my deputy, Edward Maffitt, I have had firm and courteous guidance and good judgment in the tradition of the true professional. Past experience of the staff with ambassadors has been favorable so it is favorably disposed toward us. We are, to be sure, expected to combine the best qualities of the Bowles', the Coopers and the Bunkers[13] but that ought to be easy. I am not quite sure where the line falls in this business between dignity and stuffiness. I shall try to combine decorum and discipline with a reasonably relaxed attitude toward rank but, of course, without descending to the raffish informality of the White House.

The senior officials of the Foreign Ministry are intelligent and on easy terms with the Embassy. Communication seems to involve a minimum of restraint. My first talk with Nehru was not quite so easy—I am not entirely at home in his presence and I rather wonder if anyone is. He does not take kindly to argument. One senses this and is tempted to try to avoid it. (A strong political leader is, I think, one who raises a certain moral threshold against disagreement.) He read your letter with obvious enjoyment (and later circulated it to his officials) and we talked for a bit about books, the number of bicycles as an index of progress, and other trivia. Then he turned to the Congo which is very much on his mind. His principal concern here was the delay in getting the troops from Dar es-Salaam and getting out the Belgian and white irregulars.[14] (Dayal and Timberlake came up but less centrally.)[15] I have reported on all this to the Department. One general point struck me hard. The Indian government feels that it has committed itself deeply with this contingent and is worried about it. The UN was faltering and is very important in Indian eyes and to Indian policy. The troops shored up the UN position, may well save it, but the domestic risks now seem more considerable.

We talked in Nehru's Parliament office—a smallish, rather shabby room, indifferently furnished, not far from the floor of Parliament. He is usually here when the House is sitting; this is an aspect of his determination to get parliamentary habits firmly fixed during his lifetime. The central parliament functions at least as efficiently and equably as the Senate. In the provincial capitals, however, they throw things in their moments of truth. I could not see that Nehru had aged since I saw him last—about two years ago. His face is smooth and unlined and handsome. When I left, he asked that my new role not prevent me from continuing as an economic adviser to his government. I told him I hoped it wouldn't but that my voice might now be a trifle muted.

When I was first here in 1956 the tension between the United States and India—and between Americans and Indians—was evident, palpable. Three years later in 1959, things were much easier. Now I would sense a still further relaxation—it is necessary now that at least some members of the government remind themselves that they are neutral. Things being so I doubt that I can make much of a score.

In the next letter or so I will give you among other things some working impressions of the Indian economy—I must find out whether the Central Bank is maintaining its independence or could use Martin[16]—and on some of the strengths and weaknesses of Embassy operations.

Yours faithfully,
John Kenneth Galbraith

New Delhi, India
April 27, 1961
ITS-2[17]

Dear Mr. President:

The last week wasn't the best in the history of the Frontier and I haven't found much comfort in contemplating your problems.[18] However, I think I can offer a word or two of cheer—and since you know how I felt about this adventure, as well as my mean tendencies, you won't imagine that I am glossing things over. New Delhi was, I imagine, the worst station. The papers had carried the full newspaper accounts of our Cuban involvement with all available exaggeration. There are lots of people here who love to make life difficult for us—and who think we have been doing too well these last two or three years. And, perhaps not less than the Latin Americans, the Indians see their protection (in particular to the North) in the principle of non-intervention. This attitude is a most important force in the unpowerful part of the world, where it is naturally regarded as a vital protection. The result was a bad setting and much pressure on Nehru to give us the business.

We did not escape unscathed but it was no disaster. I kept our explanations simple and short; there is nothing worse than windy arguments. At a press conference, which came as these damn things always do on the worst day, I repeated you and then contented myself with running over our history of alleged misdemeanours in undermining Cuban despots as seen by the latter from the complaints of Spain to the present. Castro I made merely the last troublesome chapter on the list.

As much by good luck as good management I saw Nehru almost every day during the business—once during a long family lunch at his house—and this helped take a great deal of the sting out of the situation. At the beginning he made a rather unhappy statement in the House. But he ended last Saturday with a speech minimising our role, stressing that no Americans had been involved and citing a point that I had urged in our conversations, namely that 100,000 Cuban refugees were bound to cause us trouble. The episode is now over. Do keep it muted at the Washington end.

In the next few days I am going to write a detailed policy paper on how to balance prospective accomplishment and risk in matters of this sort and on the realities as distinct from the slogans of social revolution. We must be more learned on these matters than we are. Would you have an eye out for these thoughts?[19]

I am engaged, these days, in making my calls on the other ambassadors. This is an incredible waste of time. As you can imagine New Delhi is not the place where (say) Peru sends its best man or the best man wants to come.[20] Paris suits the Latin and Levantine temperament better and so does New York. One Levantine, who is accredited to a half dozen Asian governments, I suspect of being in the black market and possibly in the white slave trade. As a result he does seem rather more affluent than the common run. Many of the other diplomats obviously get along on a shoestring. They live in hideous houses decorated by some expressionist of the rural Nepal school. I do note one redeeming feature: the more under-developed the country the more over-developed the women.[21] Still after meeting many of my diplomatic colleagues I think better of my old conversations with Foster Furcolo.[22] Nehru suggested that I call on the big countries because of their vanity, the small ones because of their sensibility and omit those in between. However, I shall struggle nobly on—for a while. Fulbright should know, incidentally, that the Soviet Ambassador next door, though he understands, does not speak a word of English.[23] He has given me five jars of caviar and I have given him a copy of one of my books. I hope you do as well trading with Khrushchev.

I did pick up one useful bit of information yesterday. An Indian told me that when they recently played a game of ordinary or non-touch football with the Indonesians in Djakarta, the latter got a medicine man to the stadium early in the morning to insure by incantation and other well-established techniques that the citizen-supporters of your friend Soekarno would win. I asked if it worked. My Indian friend replied, "Of course not. We had the better team and anyhow our astrologist had picked the day".

I am still looking into Embassy operations. Next week after welcoming Sarge[24] I shall give you a view of this operation.

Faithfully,
John Kenneth Galbraith

New Delhi, India
May 10, 1961

ITS-3[25]

Dear Mr. President:

The last two weeks have been very busy, mostly over Laos. The cease fire now seems firm. Thus I have my first diplomatic triumph. However, my satisfaction is slightly dimmed by the fact that at no point can I see the slightest relation between my stupendous effort and the result.[26]

I have reached two conclusions as the result of my concern with Laos and the Congo. These jungle regimes, where the writ of government runs only as far as the airport, are going to be a hideous problem for us in the months ahead. (Angola and probably Nepal are next.) The rulers do not control or particularly influence their own people; and they neither have nor warrant their people's support. As a military ally the entire Laos nation is clearly inferior to a battalion of conscientious objectors from World War I. We get nothing from their support and I must say I wonder what the Communists get. One answer, no doubt, is that the Communists will do a better job of organizing existing leaders out. Nevertheless I am convinced that in these primitive countries we cannot always back winners and we cannot be sure that the winners we back will stay on our side. For the same reason we should never assume that anyone is lost to the Communists. We must above all face the probability of gains and losses and certainly no single loss will be decisive. Most of all we must not allow ourselves or the country to imagine that gains or losses in these incoherent lands are the same as gains or losses in the organized world, that of France or Italy—or India.

A second thought I have been trying out provisionally on the Indian officials. It is that our friends must one day recognize that there has been a change in our attitude toward these regimes. In Dulles'[27] day our efforts to save them from Communism did have elements of a holy crusade. Perhaps there was occasion then for some alarm over our (or rather Dulles') zeal. But we are getting more practical. Those who get alarmed over what we do need to ask themselves whether they would prefer total inaction. Would India be happy were we to wash our hands of Nepal, South Viet Nam, or the Congo? Would they wish that we were neutrals too?

In spite of Laos and the ceremonial preoccupations of this task, I have begun to get a fair view of the operation of this Embassy. I doubt that you would wish to acquaint yourself with all features of all your Missions. But perhaps you should know about one. And India probably reveals the common strengths and weaknesses with the further advantage that it is exceedingly important in itself.

With the exception of some adventuresome and spooky enterprises[28] which do not lend themselves to these letters (but about which I will have much to say when I see you and others in June) the affairs of the Embassy can like Gaul, and most everything else, be divided into three parts: (1) the traditional political, economic and administrative tasks of the Embassy proper; (2) the technical assistance and other economic aid functions; and, (3) the United States Information Service. Two and three, i.e., technical aid and USIS are very important and very large—the largest, indeed, of any overseas headquarters.

The central Embassy staff, the whole show in your London youth, and including the political and economic ministers, counsellors and secretaries, are hard-working, competent and admirably committed to the interest of the United States without being humorlessly enslaved by any particular line or theology. They respect the Indians and are respected in turn. The political sophistication of the younger officers seems higher than when I knew the Service fifteen years ago. I am well pleased with this part of the enterprise.

The USIS runs libraries, publishes three or four magazines, distributes books, arranges exhibits, books American cultural enterprises and gets your speeches to the intellectually starving masses. It is a large operation; the current budget is $3,466,261. My impression of this is less happy. The people here are hard-working and dedicated. The various activities are conducted with reasonable efficiency. The libraries handle an enormous traffic. (At the end of the month the McGraw-Hill bakery magazine is grubby from its many avid readers.) What is missing is spirit or lift. The organization lacks excitement. Everyday tasks are not even very expertly done. The magazines and other publications are poorly written and edited with unattractive layouts and fairly dull material. Our upper middlebrow magazine is so far inferior to what the Poles distribute as to make one cry. (The latter very rarely mentions Communism and can even outstrip us on an article on ecclesiastical architecture.) The book presentation program for libraries has not, in the past, thought it wise to distribute your books or Schlesinger's[29] or even very many of mine.

Much of the trouble is from the Washington support. You cannot imagine how bad this is. Each morning, over the air, comes the day's American story. I can no longer read it for simple reasons of health; five minutes of this wireless file and one loses his breakfast and cannot eat the rest of the day. In two weeks it caused me to lose twenty pounds and I have prescribed it for the Saudi Arabian ambassador who is badly overweight. Apart from some useful speech texts it consists in equal parts of utterly irrelevant pieces about the progress of the grass silage industry; tedious and execrably written articles on the American economy (I attach today's thought which brilliantly likens the nation to a large corporation. You would have saved yourself trouble if you had held out for the Merchandise Mart)[30]—or uninspired thoughts of the lesser members of the bureaucracy, or diatribes against Communism. The latter are perhaps the dreariest feature of all. I cannot read them without pausing to consider whether the Communists have something, and Murrow may well be turning me into a security risk. Lately I have been sending him samples of this gaseous diffusion with a note of personal congratulation.[31]

I am going to need a new head of the USIS organization here. So far I have been shown only a worthy but broken-arch bureaucrat. Outsiders are opposed in the interest of upholding the merit system. I am puzzled as to why a merit system is important in the absence of merit but you are President and will understand better. Or perhaps you could ask Larry O'Brien to explain.[32]

The technical assistance program, and related economic aid activities, also produce no cheering. In the old Dulles days the Indian Government regarded the technical assistance activities— agriculture, public health, education and so forth—with considerable suspicion. It seemed an invasion of sovereignty, a possible cover for cold war penetration. And there was a feeling that some of our experts we were sending were less than leaders in their chosen fields—a suspicion that was amply confirmed when at intervals some truly remarkable stumble-bums were off-loaded at the local airport. As a consequence of all this whenever the Indian Government asked for help there was a great effort to respond—"at least they were asking us." No effort was made to fit the particular expert into a sense-making program or even to be sure that what he did made sense. And the Indians in turn subjected our talent to a scrutiny that regularly took and still takes months. So our technical assistance is a hit and miss affair, helping here and missing there, and maybe even doing occasional damage by diverting attention from first essentials. On the essentials, for example technical assistance to improve Indian agriculture, the effort is spread very, very thin—so thin that I cannot think it will have any appreciable impact before the second or possibly the third Coming. The experts range from very good and very skilled to indifferent. Vacancies remain unfilled for many months and by the time a man is cleared for appointment, if he is any good, he is no longer available. Quite a few experts still come for short tours of duty and afflict the Mission and the government with the divine revelations of every newcomer to India. It may be debated in the matter of religion but no one seems to question the doctrine of immaculate conception where ideas on economic development are involved.

The leadership of the economic and technical aid program, if not inspired, seems sound. I have already asked for a thorough restudy of its operation and I have given my thoughts on needed reform. These include concentration of our energies on first essentials, the elimination of frills, and a clear indication to the Indian Government that we will henceforth provide assistance only when it is seriously wanted. This being so we will expect our judgment on people to be accepted and will undertake to ensure performance. This means we will have to provide people of first-rate ability.

Shriver[33] was here last week and did exceedingly well. The Prime Minister liked him and he seems even to have charmed Krishna

Menon[34] whom I sent him to visit. Krishna Menon is an odd and difficult character. But some small part of the problem, I think, is that the Republicans treated him with all the warmth and tact of a Brahmin encountering a leprous untouchable at his table. I am routing all visitors through K. M.'s office.

That includes Lyndon[35] who arrives next week with two airplanes, a party of fifty, a communications unit, and other minor accoutrements of modern democracy. I will meet him in Bangkok and try to make him feel good that he was on the ticket. His trip may not be decisive for the peace of Asia. The East, as you know, is inscrutable.

> Faithfully,
> John Kenneth Galbraith

New Delhi, India
July 11, 1961

ITS-4[36]

Dear Mr. President:

I have been back about three weeks and from day to day I have been planning to pass along some thoughts on matters in Washington and here. I must say that the trip was reasonably exhausting with my time divided almost equally between asking for things that I needed and asking not to have things that I don't need. On occasion I am appalled at the money possessed by the United States Government for things that aren't necessary. A few more years and I could easily become as penurious as I learn you already are.

Thus I have just successfully arrested a Commerce plan to send a high level trade mission to India—officials, businessmen, staff to spend several weeks touring India to acquaint the natives[37] with the virtues of American products. They do not sell, only expound. It was all but settled when I learned about it. I discover that there have been six such missions in the last six years. I learn further that the results of all have been nil or negative except as described by the participants or the unduly polite. The Indians operate a watertight system of exchange control and import licenses, with our encouragement, to save dollars. However admirable American goods they cannot be bought without a license and licenses are available only to the extent that dollars are. Some dollars do get spent in other countries not because of ignorance but because our goods are too expensive. The cost of our goods, incidentally, is the major problem of our trade and our balance-of-payments. Ultimately it will be the major problem of our foreign policy for the latter costs a lot of money which we must earn.

I do discover that past missions have raised hopes in the minds of numerous Indian entrepreneurs that they might be allowed to import our gear grinders and garter belts—"The Americans must know what they are doing"—only to have their hopes dashed when they sought the licenses. So much for this. I cite it not for its importance but as an example of excessive affluence.

As you may have seen from my cables I discharged your commissions with Nehru on Berlin and testing and, I think, made some impression.[38] More on testing than Berlin, I think. The press dust-up over a new China policy started just as I got back so I concluded that I had better postpone any talk with the Chinese (Com) Ambassador.[39] There is an off chance that it might have become known with muddying effect. When it seems safe I will raise the matter.

From here the discussions over Berlin have an Alice-in-Wonderland quality which, sadly, I can only suppose is improved by distance. When I wonder about our ability to conduct a successful foreign policy, which is often, it is usually because of our tendency to take an issue and simplify it to the point of absurdity. The two favorite absurdities consist (1) in reducing all matters to a choice between whether we win or lose and (2) to whether we are hard or soft.

In Laos, for example, our problem has long been to escape from an impossible position with a certain amount of grace.[40] Any escape will be good and one may still be possible. But according to the official simplifiers, we have already suffered an overwhelming loss. We never, so far as I can see, had a chance to win—not anyhow since we arrived. And if we are convinced we have lost I can't see how the Communists can fail to take the hint.

In the Berlin discussions the simplification is between hard and soft. Nothing could be more irrelevant. Were the Russians determined to have a war they could doubtless force one upon us. And similarly if we were so bent. So at some point we are both hard. There is no need to demonstrate this point for it is evident. Since the contingency is one which presumably we both seek to avoid the problem is to find a solution tolerable to us in between.

Those who talk about hard solutions divert all thought from solutions by asking only that we advertise our willingness to risk a deep thermonuclear burn. In their souls they know that this is an eventuality which a President cannot accept. And they always protect themselves with their public by saying that, of course, it won't really happen. So they happily exploit the antipathy toward the Russians, strike impressively heroic poses, feel personally secure nonetheless and, when the inevitable bargain is struck, are free to condemn it as a defeat. It is only when one spells it out that one comes to realise how tactically unassailable are those who argue such tactics. I can't think that you find them very helpful.

This brings me to my suggestion of the day. In making appointments there are three qualifications which, in one way or another, rate a measure of consideration. These are *ability, political acceptability* and *personal loyalty*. It is my impression that in key positions you have put more or less the inevitable stress on political acceptability and that you have stressed ability at the expense of personal loyalty. I would not argue that ability is a wholly negligible asset. But it is often combined with a tendency to think of one's self first, one's agency second and the President last. In the end the best Roosevelt men were not the smartest but those who thought of FDR first and themselves and their agencies second. Hopkins,[41] a man of second class wit, was a case in point. At this distance I have difficulty in appreciating your use of Dean Acheson.[42] He is able. He has reestablished himself politically with the right. But I cannot think he is capable of loyalty. He will be a source of trouble for he wants the policy that serves his ego not your needs.

I suspect in these days it is almost as important to know what isn't serious as to know what is. The current flare-up in Pakistan of which you will be getting an earful strikes me as unserious. Kashmir is an involved and troublesome matter with no solution in sight but I think most of the present flare-up is political posturing.[43]

On the other hand South Viet Nam is exceedingly bad. I hope, incidentally, that your information from there is good and I have an uneasy feeling that what comes in regular channels is very bad. Unless I am mistaken Diem[44] has alienated his people to a far greater extent than we allow ourselves to know. This is our old mistake. We take the ruler's word and that of our own people who have become committed to him. The opponents are thieves and bandits; the problem is to get the police. I am sure the problem in Viet Nam is partly the means to preserve law and order. But I fear that we have one more government which, on present form, no one will support.

The monsoon has come and it is wet and almost cool. I am starting out next week to make a tour of the major cities and a few speeches. I am avoiding the Indo-American societies, the Rotary Clubs and the other usual American fora to see if I can make some dent on the university audiences. These are influential and also rather suspicious.

Yours faithfully,
John Kenneth Galbraith

New Delhi, India
July 25, 1961

ITS-5[45]

Dear Mr. President:

This has nothing to do with India. It is on the European Common Market which bothers me a lot whenever I think about it.[46] My recent thoughts have been inspired by Thorneycroft[47] who has just been here to persuade the Indians to make sacrifices they cannot afford so that Britain can join. The British are looking to their own interest; so is everyone else except ourselves. We are looking after the interests of other people. On the Common Market liberals and conservatives are divided in a peculiar way: liberals want to do the wrong thing for the wrong reasons; conservatives want to do the wrong thing for no reason at all.

The drive for European unity caught the liberal imagination in the Marshall Plan days. Partly it was to expedite European recovery and make our aid more efficient. Partly it seemed a way of erecting a new position of anti-Communist power west of the Elbe. It has rolled on under this latter banner ever since. We applaud and encourage. But we view it as a political and economic initiative peculiar to Europe which has no direct meaning for us. It is a unique act of political creation.

There is another possible view which is that modern industry with its ever increasing scale requires larger and larger trading areas. And access to markets is now more important than protection from competitors. Social security and modern fiscal policy provide the cushioning effect on national economies which were once provided much more imperfectly by tariffs. Low-wage competition such as that of Japan or Hong Kong is still inconvenient. So is *too big* a competitive impact such as could be registered by the United States. But within limits market access is now the thing. This the Common Market provides for Europeans. So viewed the ECE is not a unique act of political creation. It is an accommodation to the facts of modern economic and industrial life.

Such it is in my view. It is a reflection of a trend and Europeans are on the trend and we are not. They are developing market access at our expense. As their internal tariffs disappear they will have duty-free products from each other in competition with our duty-paid imports. No European will pay duty on (say) an American automobile when he wants a foreign car. He can have one from another Common Market country duty free. In the averaging of the internal tariffs we will also get the short end. The low-tariff countries where we now sell will be averaging up their tariffs; the countries with a tariff we cannot beat and where we have no market will be averaging down. Still we say fine. Let us get Britain and the rest of Europe in. Thus we build up Europe against the Bolshevists. In fact we are building up Europe, which is already economically powerful, against the United States.

We must react very soon. The British, once almost as retarded as we are, have seen what is happening. After using the Commonwealth for years as an excuse for keeping out of Europe they now have their best political PR types deployed around the world explaining that British interests now require the sacrifice of Commonwealth preferences for the good of Britain. We must be equally concerned. We cannot continue this policy of ignoring our own interest. I have never been worried about the Pope running the government but I am genuinely bothered about St. Francis.

We cannot and should not block the ECE. Nor is there anything to the idea of organizing our own hemisphere trading community—there isn't enough to organize. To pull in our horns and put up our tariffs as our conservatives would recommend would be fatal. So all that remains is to find a tolerable association with the Common

Market. This we must do and we must do it while we can still bargain. I am not quite prepared to say what the form of association should be, but I have some ideas which, at some juncture, I would like to offer. Ahead and required will be some hard and clear-headed trading with our allies. We cannot continue to think first of Europe or forswear any steps that might upset the present equilibrium or De Gaulle.[48]

The other day Thorneycroft asked me if I thought you could be persuaded, at some juncture, to ask De Gaulle to admit Britain. I didn't answer for you but I did take the liberty of telling him that henceforth we would have to look seriously to our own interest. He was obviously shocked but took it well.

This letter, incidentally, is one of the dividends (or stock assessments) of the new air lift. I am writing it en route from New Delhi to Madras with the monsoon far below. It couldn't be done in a Dakota.[49]

> Yours faithfully,
> John Kenneth Galbraith

New Delhi, India
August 15, 1961

ITS-6[50]

Dear Mr. President:

I have a variety of matters of interest and amusement including a few of the subtleties in self-advertisement which you must be finding familiar in your communications. I might number them:

(1) I trust your life was suitably enriched by your visit with Baruch.[51] I appreciate your seeing the old fraud and it liquidates a campaign promise. However, he should not be allowed to think that the best things in life, including visits to the White House, are free. He never used to.

(2) We have just had a three day meeting with Bowles plus one with Talbot.[52] I was admirably instructed on what I already knew, didn't believe or couldn't remember. I can't say that you have done wonders for Chet's morale. In what Lyndon, in his inimitable English calls a belly-to-belly talk I told him to go home, stop talking,

write no more memoranda and concentrate on making the African, Asian and Latino parts of the Department work. He thinks he has aroused bureaucratic enmities by firing too many people; I said it was my impression he had aroused yours by not firing enough. (Even the Attorney-General would have winced at all the candor.) Chet promised to do his best but says he is boxed. In government people get boxed only when they won't kick their way out. I like Bowles. His only trouble is an uncontrollable instinct for persuasion which he brings to bear on the persuaded, the unpersuaded and the totally irredeemable alike. In my view the State Department needs not to be persuaded but to be told. I think it conceivable that Chet might take hold. He was very good in OPA.[53]

(3) If the State Department drives you crazy you might calm yourself by contemplating its effect on me. The other night I woke with a blissful feeling and discovered I had been dreaming that the whole Goddamn place had burned down. I dozed off again hoping for a headline saying no survivors. I think I dislike most the uncontrollable instinct for piously reasoned inaction. When the Department does respond to telegrams it is invariably to recommend evasion of issues that cannot be evaded. The result, in the end, is that we get the worst of all available worlds. The touchiest issue here is the shipment of military hardware to Pakistan—arming the present rival and foe and the ancient enemy and rulers of the Hindus. A few weeks ago one of our aircraft carriers brought twelve supersonic jets to Karachi where they were unloaded in all the secrecy that would attend mass sodomy on the BMT at rush hour. Rumors plus Indian intelligence raised the number to 30, then 50, then 75. (This, I learn, is escalation.) The Pakistanis asked that the number not be released in order to keep the Indians in doubt and the Department agreed over my protests. When the thing promised to get out of hand here the Department cabled me sympathy. Eventually I wrung authority to release the number out of Talbot more or less by physical violence. That then double-crossed the Paks who had been promised we wouldn't tell.

Talbot, who was here with Bowles, spent some hours outlining the excellent longer range studies that are now under way on our foreign policy. They are being conducted in a cooperative spirit; he says, indeed, that complete harmony prevails. I think he has a good sense of tactics. He took a cautious line on the Pentagon but came out strongly for keeping the Peace Corps in its place.

(4) I liked very much your reference to national interest in your statement on the common market. However I remain unhappy. The British accession will convert the ECM from a step toward political unification, which is the liberal's image, to a tariff club that discriminates systematically against our products. Yet the magic of the word unification will keep us from demanding the concessions the British will get. No one seems to see that we have a large and expensive foreign policy in which money serves as a substitute for intelligence and that we must have the export earnings to pay for it. Indeed we haven't really been paying for it for years—instead we have been drawing systematically on accumulated reserves.

(5) I have just completed a tour of the major Indian cities with an incredible variety of activities including a major speech to the University students in each place. I had large, interested and friendly crowds and the talks, which were on economic policy and planning, went exceedingly well and are still being much discussed. In short your well-known political prescience is again justified and I am a considerable success.

(6) Laos continues to command a lot of my time. I am trying hard to persuade the Indians that once we accept neutrality they cannot be less concerned to protect it than we. If neutrality means that Laos goes to the Communists, the word will stink and everyone will attribute the failure to acceptance of an Indian policy. It is an uphill fight. The Department expects me to explain our devotion to neutrality in Laos one day and our supersonic toys for the Pakistanis the next. That is called a policy. The Indian habit of mediating is strong—halfway between the United States and Russia is somehow right—and Krishna Menon[54] is also a major stumbling block. I don't think he is open to persuasion for he owes his position to his hold on the left wing of the Congress Party. But even were he open to conviction I would rather work on Wayne Morse.[55] Incidentally, I find Menon the most interesting man in the top hierarchy. I have rarely encountered a politician who is more completely exempt from the wish to be loved.

(7) Two weeks ago I went to Geneva for two or three days to get some more ammunition. I asked Arthur to tell you what a good job Harriman is doing—the really right combination of patience, firmness and dignity and good sense.[56] We have a depressingly weak hand to play and I sometimes wonder why we should expect the

Communists to turn in their winning cards. Maybe they are tired of the Laos.

(8) From here I get the impression that your position on Berlin makes a great deal of sense. I predict an outcome that will reflect credit on you and your Administration.

Faithfully,
John Kenneth Galbraith

New Delhi, India
August 26, 1961[57]

PERSONAL AND SECRET

Dear Mr. President:

I am a good deal worried about our negotiating position on admission of the Chinese Communists to the United Nations. I know as a politician rather than as a diplomat exactly how difficult this situation is and how difficult you know it to be. Indeed some years ago I concluded that I would speak my mind on what I deemed to be inevitable and have had some experience of the consequences. I am not reacting now to the merits of the case but to the reputation and posture of the Administration and the United States.

The experts have cooked up a device which they think will keep the Chicoms[58] out for another year. This, as you certainly know, is to have Chinese representation made an "important question" which, if adopted by a majority vote, would make the decision to change from Formosa to Peking subject to a two-third majority vote. The tactic is patently transparent. Debate over whether it is an "important question" will straightaway become a debate on admission. We will have gone out on a limb for what seems to be a clever maneuver and will be defeated. At the meeting of South Asian Ambassadors a fortnight ago not a soul thought we could promote a majority for exclusion. This morning Maffitt, my DCM, and I discussed the tactic with Desai at the Foreign Office.[59] Since I could easily be considered a prejudiced party I let Maffitt carry the ball which he did very cleverly. He got nowhere. Desai simply said, "There would have to be a majority vote and it is our position that the seat belongs to the Chinese mainland." He was willing to consider charter revision as an interesting idea. But this tactic would greatly alarm me for it would give the Russians a hunting license on the office of Secretary-General.

As I say, I see no chance of lining up a majority. What seems to me inevitable is that we shall have a minority consisting of the more dubious figures in the world—Salazar, Chiang, Sarit.[60] We won't have Ayub.[61] The New Frontier will get credit only for continuing the Old Frontier policy with the difference that with us it failed. And even should we win, we will have the issue back with us again a year hence and an election to boot. There is no happy solution to this problem but wise men have long been told of the proper reaction to inevitable rape. I would urge that we take a passive attitude on the Chicoms, making a token vote against them but no impassioned pleas. Our prestige should not be put on the block. Then let us put our energies into keeping Formosa in the General Assembly. Here we are acting on behalf of an old ally and no one will doubt our good will. We might even get a majority for this although I confess to being uncertain about the precise legal procedures.

I have put all these matters in a pointed telegram to the State Department. The result was not entirely disappointing. It produced one of the rudest responses in the history of diplomacy.

Yours faithfully,
John Kenneth Galbraith

New Delhi, India
September 19, 1961

ITS-7[62]

Dear Mr. President:
Here are some thoughts on the perils of our time, some of which follow the line of our conversation the other morning. You must have discovered that I am considerably less incoherent on paper than in oral exercise, the mark I imagine of a deep but turgid mind.

There is a tendency in Washington to conclude that any serious problem must be infinitely complex. This has never been more in evidence than in the case of Berlin.[63] I can't but think that the Berlin issue is rather simple: the Russians may (1) be concerned with building up the prestige of the East German regime, holding people there, giving it a regular existence and cutting down the general impact of our presence in West Berlin. Or (2) they may be concerned with denying our access and throwing our soldiers out. If the first is their aim things will be worked out. If they intend the second we will have a nasty time—but I don't suggest it will be war except by accident but there will be a lengthy trial of nerves and strength since we both are after the same thing.

In a world where everyone else is sure what the Russians want, I have learned, painfully, to keep an open mind. My guess is, given the weakness of the East German regime and the willingness of the Russians to talk about access and token troops, that the Russians want the first alternative. (Writing to Nehru a few weeks ago Khrushchev said he could not stand the collapse of the East German government and in Moscow the other day when Nehru said he did not think much of the Ulbricht government[64] Khrushchev said in substance, "Neither do we".)

Access and presence are important to us. Accordingly we should ask for what we have plus the removal of all doubts and irritations connected therewith. Thus my notion of a free and open road into Berlin along which all can travel without let or hindrance with similar security for air, water and rail travel and transport. Where we are on firm ground and our need is clear we should ask, and ask a lot. We shouldn't ask for what we don't have and won't get.

This has a heavy bearing on our position on East Germany. It is now a Washington cliche that we won't go to war over East Germany. But I hold it even more important that our prestige—either that of the country or the Administration—not be put at risk on this issue. It pains me to hear talk about reunification and self-determination for the East Germans as bargaining points. No one can bargain with what he doesn't have except Chiang Kai-shek.[65] All this effort does is build up the importance of what the Soviets will get. We invent a defeat and make it look as bad as possible.

That is why I come out with the idea of a time limit. Let us accept and even (if possible) mildly welcome the idea of a regular status for East Germany in the short run while making it clear that reunification is essential in the long run. And in exceptionally rigorous pursuit of my exceptionally rigorous logic let us make this clear in advance and not reserve it as a bargaining point. Then we won't set up a defeat for ourselves.

So much for Germany. When I wake up at night I worry that in our first year in office we will be credited with losing Laos which we did not have, losing East Berlin which we did not have, losing East Germany which we did not have and (touchy point) with failing to persuade the world that Formosa is China. As an extreme idealist I am in favor of lost causes. But I wonder if we should lose our lost causes more than once.

In coming back to Washington I was struck with how sensible and flexible are the views on the top side of the State Department, not to mention the White House, as compared with those which come to me in the telegrams. And in Washington itself reassurance disappears as one gets to what by some witticism is called the working level. It is very important, indeed absolutely indispensable, that we begin to understand what is wrong with the Department.

It is not that people are dull although quite a few are. Nor are they exceptionally conservative although there is a widespread feeling that God ordained some individuals to make foreign policy without undue interference from presidents or politicians. The far more serious problem is that the Department is simply too large. And with size has come an inflexibility that is as inevitable as it is incredible. The reason is simple: there are more people on C Street than there are problems. Nothing is so serious for a crypto-Talleyrand as unemployment. By common understanding, therefore, everyone insists on, and by common consent everyone is accorded, a finger in every important pie. Every civilized group acts in some degree by unanimous consent. So one cannot get agreement on anything new. When a deadline approaches everyone repairs hurriedly to what was agreed several years ago. Accordingly the sheer size of the Department freezes it to all of its antique positions.

The problem here is a serious one. Nothing in my view is so important as to get the Department back to manageable size. The Pentagon is not nearly so bad. For while it is larger and much too large most everyone is concerned with operational problems. In State the multitude must all make policy. When I was back this time one of my assistant secretary friends attended the Secretary's staff meeting from nine-fifteen till ten. Then he had a meeting with the

Under Secretary on operations until ten-thirty. Then he took until eleven-thirty to inform his staff of what went on at the earlier meetings. Whereupon they adjourned to pass on the news to their staffs. This is, I am told, communication.

Faithfully,
John Kenneth Galbraith

New Delhi, India
October 9, 1961

ITS-8[66]

Dear Mr. President:

I keep seeing stories that we are to have a serious review of foreign policy. Men of wisdom will applaud this. When things are not good, it is usually imagined that a review, or possibly a reorganization, will make them better. No one ever asks whether the best is being made of a lousy situation. That, on the whole, is my present view of things. However, a good review will create a lot of needed employment for the State Department.

I am sure most people exaggerate the scope for change in foreign policy. The greatest difficulty with Dulles[67] was his yearning for new and exciting variants in policy—massive retaliation, the thumbed nose at neutrals, military alliances with the indigent—that were change for the sake of change. They were partly change for the sake of putting on a black tie and proclaiming a new policy to a gathering of the affluent in Manhattan.

Foreign policy, like domestic policy, is a reflection of the fundamental instincts of those who make it. All of us have been reared with the same instincts, more or less—that we should combine courtesy with compassion, suspect pompous or heroic stances, respect our capacity to negotiate, refuse to be pushed and seek solutions in social stability rather than military prowess. Since these instincts cannot be changed not much can be done about the policy that derives from them.

The country is indeed fortunate that our instincts are sound.

I do worry a good deal about the domestic political position in which our foreign policy will be placing us. Ahead of us, in fact, are the same difficulties that beset the Truman Era. The right, in the United States, will always criticize reasonableness as softness. To be sensible is to appease. And to knock the Soviets or the Chicoms into the gutter is not the least bit warlike. It is the only thing they understand and respect. Democrats are warlike because they are weak-kneed.

The Truman Administration never developed a way of dealing with this dialectic. Sometimes it brought Republicans, including Dulles, into the Administration with the hope that this would blunt the attack. Sometimes it tried to show that it could talk as pugnaciously as the Republicans. Neither worked.

The answer, I am sure, is to pin the label of warrior firmly on these goons. This is not an emotional reaction but a sound political tactic to which they are vulnerable. When they speak of total victory they invite total annihilation. They aren't brave but suicidal. There is a curious superficial pugnacity about the American people which, I am persuaded, does not go very deep. They applaud the noisy man but they reconsider if they think him dangerous. We must, I feel, make it clear that these men are dangerous. They survive because we have let them have the best of both worlds: they could appeal to the pugnacity as a defender of the peace.

These are matters which, of course, should be handled by craftsmen below your office. One of the major problems with foreign policy, as distinct from domestic policy, is the silence it imposes on almost all of its defenders. Secretaries, undersecretaries and ambassadors, the natural debaters on these matters, are all silenced by tradition plus the myth of bipartisanship. So the attackers have it all to themselves. Sometimes I would like to offer some thoughts on how to even up the game.

Bipartisanship, incidentally, is a booby trap for Democrats. We make concessions to the Republicans and appoint them to office. We refrain from nailing the extremists to their nonsense. We mute our own defense or stand down. And, in the end, not only Goldwater but Eisenhower does not hesitate to attack. Cuba is a classic case.

I am going to Calcutta on Monday to identify myself with the efforts to rehabilitate this hideous community. If the Communists were not so stupid it could incubate enough for all Asia. Then I am starting on a 10 or 12 day tour of the far South; a major speech and honorary degree at one of the southern universities, inauguration of a school feeding program in Kerala, a general show of support for the non-Communist forces in this state, a speech at the Defence College in Wellington, a breathtaking display of horsemanship, a visit to the Maharajah of Mysore and the great religious festival of Dasara, an inspection of two industrial plants in Bangalore. When I return it will be almost time to come back for Nehru's visit.[68] I am preceding him by about a week. The Department is preparing a vast number of special papers for you. I think you can safely forego the pleasure and get the whole thing from the highest authority.

I remember once during the war Henderson[69] sent a great bale of memoranda to the President on price legislation. A little later [there was] a meeting in the White House and the President said:

"Leon, what about the constitutionality of this legislation and why isn't Labor included?"

Henderson said, "Mr. President, I sent you memoranda on both of those points."

Roosevelt said, "Leon, are you laboring under the impression that I read these memoranda of yours? I can't even lift them."

Although at times I have been rather troubled by Berlin, I have always had the feeling that it would be worked out. I have continued to worry far, far more about South Viet Nam. This is more complex, far less controllable, far more varied in the factors involved, far more susceptible to misunderstanding. And to make matters worse, I have no real confidence in the sophistication and political judgment of our people there. Harriman, incidentally, shares my view.

Yours faithfully,
John Kenneth Galbraith

TOP SECRET [telegram]
For the President from Ambassador Galbraith
Policy in Vietnam
From John Kenneth Galbraith

1. Here is my full analysis of our problem and course in South Vietnam. From my stay there, talks at Cincpac[70] and Bangkok, previous reading of the traffic and experience of the region I feel reasonably sure of my ground. You will be aware of the intense theological disputes which rage over such issues as the political position of Diem, the scope of external support to the insurrection and others. Where a solution of these is not relevant to a practical course of action I have not entered the debate. I have also endeavored to work from the circumstances to the action rather than the more customary procedure which is to move from the preferred course of action back to the circumstances. Where my bias intrudes, as in the case of troop commitment, I have made it clear.

2. The Viet Cong[71] insurrection is still growing in effect. The outbreak on the northern highlands is matched by a potentially even more damaging impact on the economy and especially on the movement of rice to Saigon.

3. In the absence of knowledge of the admixture of terror and economic and social evangelism we had best assume that it is employing both. We must not forever be guided by those who misunderstand the dynamics of revolution and imagine that because the Communists do not appeal to us they are abhorrent to everyone.

4. In our enthusiasm to prove outside intervention before world opinion we have unquestionably exaggerated the role of material assistance especially in the main area of insurrection in the far south. That leaders and radio guidance come in we know. But the amount of ammunition and weaponry that a man can carry on his back for several hundred kilometers over jungle trails was not increased appreciably by Marx. No major conflict can depend on such logistic support.

5. A maximum of 18,000 lightly armed men are involved in the insurrection. These are GVN[72] estimates and the factor of exaggeration is unquestionably considerable. Ten thousand is more probable. What we have in opposition involves a heavy theological

dispute. Diem it is said is a great but defamed leader.[73] It is also said he has lost touch with the masses, is in political disrepute and otherwise no good. This debate can be bypassed by agreed points. It is agreed that administratively Diem is exceedingly bad. He holds far too much power in his own hands, employs his army badly, has no intelligence organization worthy of the name, has arbitrary or incompetent subordinates in the provinces and, some achievements notwithstanding, has a poor economic policy. He has also effectively resisted improvement for a long while in face of heavy deterioration. This is enough. Whether his political posture is nepotic, despotic, out of touch with the villagers and hence damaging or whether this damage is the figment of Saigon intellectuals does not bear on our immediate policy and may be by-passed at least in part.

6. The SVN[74] army numbers 170,000 and with paramilitary units of the civil guard and home defense forces a quarter of a million. Were this well deployed on behalf of an effective government it should be obvious that the Viet Cong would have no chance of success or takeover. Washington is currently having an intellectual orgasm on the unbeatability of guerrilla war. Were guerrillas effective in a ratio of one to fifteen or twenty-five it is obvious that no government would be safe. The Viet Cong, it should be noted, is strongest in the southern delta which is not jungle but open rice paddy.

7. The fundamental difficulties in countering the insurgency, apart from absence of intelligence, are two-fold. First is the poor command, deployment, training, morale and other weaknesses of the army and paramilitary forces. And second while they can operate—sweep—through any part of the country and clear out any visible insurgents, they cannot guarantee security afterwards. The Viet Cong comes back and puts the arm on all who have collaborated. This fact is very important in relation to requests for American manpower. Our forces would conduct the round-up operations which the RVN[75] army can already do. We couldn't conceivably send enough men to provide safety for the villages as a substitute for an effectively trained civil guard and home defense force and, perhaps, a politically cooperative community.

8. The key and inescapable point, then, is the ineffectuality (abetted debatably by the unpopularity) of the Diem government. This is the strategic factor. Nor can anyone accept the statement of those who have been either too long or too little in Asia that his is the

inevitable posture of the Asian mandarin. For one thing it isn't true, but were it so the only possible conclusion would be that there is no future for mandarins. The Communists don't favor them.

9. I come now to a lesser miscalculation, the alleged weakening emphasis of the Mekong flood. Floods in this part of the world are an old trap for western non-agriculturists. They are judged by what the Ohio does to its towns. Now as the flood waters recede it is already evident that this flood conforms to the Asian pattern, one repeated every year in India. The mud villages will soon grow again. Some upland rice was drowned because the water rose too rapidly. Nearer the coast the pressure on the brackish water will probably bring an offsetting improvement. Next year's crop will be much better for the silt.

10. I come now to policy, first the box we are in partly as the result of recent moves and second how we get out without a take-over. We have just proposed to help Diem in various ways in return for a promise of administrative and political reforms. Since the administrative (and possibly political) ineffectuality are the strategic factors for success the ability to get reforms is decisive. With them the new aid and gadgetry will be useful. Without them the helicopters, planes and advisers won't make an appreciable difference.

11. In my completely considered view, as stated yesterday, Diem will not reform either administratively or politically in any effective way. That is because he cannot. It is politically naive to expect it. He senses that he cannot let power go because he would be thrown out. He may disguise this even from himself with the statement that he lacks effective subordinates but the circumstance remains unchanged. He probably senses that his greatest danger is from the army. Hence the reform that will bring effective use of his manpower, though the most urgent, may be the most improbable.

12. The political reforms are even more unlikely but the issue is academic. Once the image of a politician is fixed, whether among opposition intellectuals or peasants, it is not changed. Nor do politicians change themselves. Diem's image would not be changed by his taking in other non-Communists, initiating some social reforms or otherwise meeting the requirements of our demarche.

13. However, having started on this hopeless game we have no alternative but to play it out for a minimum time. Those who think there is hope of reform will have to be persuaded. Since there is no chance of success we must do two things to protect our situation.

One is to make clear, as I suggested previously, that our commitment is to results and not to promises since Diem is experienced in both promising without performing and in providing the shadow without the substance of performance. And we can press hardest in the area of army reform where the needed changes are most specific and most urgent. The likelihood of fundamental progress given Diem's suspicion of the army is, however, not great.

14. Ambassador Nolting and General McGarr,[76] both heavily identified with this pressure for reform should remain to press their case. Though acting loyally, Nolting is not happy about the effect of pressure on Diem. He believes rather that we should lend him our prestige and power while working more gradually for reform. This policy by my analysis would merely confirm Diem in his inadequacy, a risk which Nolting concedes. If our prestige would have provided the security for reform we would have had results long before now.

15. It follows from my reasoning that the only solution must be to drop Diem. Korea represents the only model that holds out any promise whatever for us. Without doubt Diem was a significant figure in his day. But he has run his course. He cannot be rehabilitated. Incidentally this view is held independently by the senior political counsellor of our embassy, the man who has been longest in Vietnam.

16. In my view, and this is necessarily speculative, dropping Diem will be neither difficult nor unduly dangerous. The Viet Cong are in position to cause trouble widely over the country. That is far from meaning that they are able with their small number to take over and control the country. The army if ineffective is thought to be non-Communist. The rumors of coups are endemic. Nolting while not in favor has said that a nod from the United States would be influential. At the earliest moment that it becomes evident that Diem will not and cannot implement in any real way the reforms Washington has requested we should make it quietly clear that we are withdrawing our support from him as an individual. His day would then I believe be over. While no one can promise a safe transaction we are now married to failure.

17. It is a cliche that there is no alternative to Diem's regime. This is politically naive. Where one man has dominated the scene for good or ill there never seems to be. No one considered Truman an alternative to Roosevelt. There is none for Nehru. There was none I

imagine for Rhee.[77] This is an optical illusion arising from the fact that the eye is fixed on the visible figures. It is a better rule that nothing succeeds like successors.

18. We should not be alarmed by the army as an alternative. It would buy time and get a fresh dynamic. It is not ideal; civilian rule is ordinarily more durable and more saleable to the world. But a change and a new start is of the essence and in considering opinion we may note that Diem's flavor is not markedly good in Asia.

19. A time of crisis in our policy on South Vietnam will come when it becomes evident that the reforms for which we have asked have not come off and that our presently proferred aid is not accomplishing anything. Troops will be urged to back up Diem. It will be sufficiently clear that I think this must be resisted. Our soldiers would not deal with the vital weakness. They could perpetuate it. They would enable Diem to continue to concentrate on protecting his own position at the expense of countering the insurgency. Last spring, following the vice-president's promise of more aid, proposals for increased and reformed taxes which were well advanced were promptly dropped. The parallel on administrative and political reform could be close.

20. It will be said that we need troops for a show of strength and determination in the area. Since the troops will not deal with fundamental faults—since there can't be enough of them to give security to the countryside—their failure to provide security could create a worse crisis of confidence. You will be aware of my general reluctance to move in troops. On the other hand I would note that it is those of us who have worked in the political vineyard and who have committed our hearts most strongly to the political fortunes of the New Frontier who worry most about its bright promise being sunk under the rice fields. Dulles in 1954 saw the dangers in this area.[78] Dean Acheson knew he could not invest men in Chiang.[79]

21. We should press forward on the diplomatic front to get all possible international support for our position and to raise the barrier to more overt Hanoi intervention as high as possible. This was always a long shot. As the result of my trip I think it a longer one. That is because the actual material support is smaller than our propaganda has persuaded us to believe and I don't suppose we can stop the moral support and leadership which the insurrection receives. However, we should make all effort.

22. In this connection, in addition to the other moves at Geneva,

on the ICC[80] and through the Indians to Hanoi as discussed we should ask our NATO ally the Canadians and our [ANZUS] ally the Australians to make clear to the Chinese the importance we attach to peace in this area. There can no longer be any question that the food these two are supplying is of nearly desperate importance to the Chinese. I verified the point further in long talks in Hong Kong. Properly approached the Canadians and Australians would surely make the point forcefully.

23. As I have said the present game must be played most with the present diplomatic and military leadership. Under no circumstances should there be any impairment of the civilian leadership by interposition of a new high-ranking general. When policy changes on Diem it will be time to change the leadership. In the next few weeks economic factors will become increasingly critical and there is now no one in the country with an adequate grasp of these issues or the power to deal firmly with Washington. Someone of undoubted ability in this field—Eugene Staley[81] if he can be drafted or Jack Bell[82] if Guatemala can wait—should be sent forthwith. In the military field we will have an up-to-date program of reforms for putting in the day Diem goes. We are not as well situated on the economic and social side and the situation here is changing rapidly.

24. My overall feeling is that despite the error implicit in this last move and the supposition that Diem can be reformed, the situation is not hopeless. It is only hopeless if we marry our course to that of a man who must spend more time protecting his own position and excluding those who threaten it than in fighting the insurgency. Diem's calculation instinctive or deliberate is evident. He has already been deposed once and not by the Communists. He can see his clear and present danger as well as anyone.[83]

ITS-9[84]

Dear Mr. President:

You will already have had sundry more official communications from me on South Viet Nam. This is by way of giving you something of the informal flavor and color of the local scene.

It is certainly a can of snakes. I am reasonably accustomed to oriental government and politics, but I was not quite prepared for Diem. As you will doubtless be warned, whenever anyone reaches an inconvenient conclusion on this country, he has been duped. My view is derived neither from the Indians nor the Saigon intellectuals but my personal capacity for error. One of the proposals which I am told was made to Max Taylor[85] provides an interesting clue to our man.[86] It was that a helicopter be provided to pluck him out of his palace and take him directly to the airport. This is because his surface travel through Saigon requires the taking in of all laundry along the route, the closing of all windows, an order to the populace to keep their heads in, the clearing of all streets, and a vast bevy of motorcycle outriders to protect him on his dash. Every trip to the airport requires such arrangements and it is felt that a chopper would make him seem more democratic. Incidentally, if Diem leaves town for a day, all members of his cabinet are required to see him off and welcome him back although this involves less damage to efficiency than might be supposed.

The political reality is the stasis which arises from his greater need to protect himself from a coup than to protect the country from the Viet Cong. I am quite clear that the absence of intelligence, the centralization of Army control, the incredible dual role of the provincial governors as Army generals and political administrators, the subservient incompetence of the latter, are all related to his fear, perhaps quite subjective, of being given the heave.

The desire to prolong one's days in office has a certain consistency the world around and someday somebody should explain this to the State Department with pictures. I would love to have come up with the conclusion that our man would be reformed and made into an effective military and political force. It would have given me similar hopes for Bob Wagner.[87]

Saigon has a curious aspect. It is a rather shabby version of a

French provincial city—say, Toulouse as I remember it. Life proceeds normally and it has the most stylish women in all Asia. They are tall with long legs, high breasts and wear white silk pajamas and a white silk robe, split at the sides to the armpits to give the effect of a flat panel fore and aft. On a bicycle or scooter they look very compelling and one is reminded once again that an Ambassadorship is the greatest inducement to celibacy since the chastity belt. Restaurants, night clubs and hotels flourish as they seem always to do in cities of in extremis. Yet one moves around with an armed guard and a group of gunmen following in a car behind. The morale of the Americans seems to be rather good although I wonder a little bit about our technical assistance program. The people assigned to the country are confined almost exclusively to Saigon since travel has become too dangerous. I can't imagine that the agriculturists, for example, are of much value under these circumstances. The Ambassador there, a decent man who is trying to obey orders, has been treated abominably by the State Department. He first heard of Max Taylor's mission on the radio. He had no chance to comment on the orders resulting therefrom. I would reluctantly tell you who is responsible for this management were steps taken to overcome my natural grace and charity.

I liked both your Seattle and Los Angeles speeches.[88] People were rather waiting for a word against wild men and even here I heard quite a number of relieved comments. It is necessary, as I think I argued once before, to nail these people as dangerous and warlike and once this has been done they wither rapidly. In the past they have had it both ways. They could appeal to the heroic stance so beloved by our countrymen and at the same time say that theirs was the path to peace.

Incidentally, I would urge that the radical right be kept in perspective. I have a feeling that at any given time about three million Americans can be had for any militant reaction against law, decency, the Constitution, the Supreme Court, compassion and the rule of reason. They will follow Huey Long, Bill Lemke, Gerald L. K. Smith, Father Coughlin, Fritz Kuhn, Joe McCarthy, Barry Goldwater depending entirely on who is leading at the moment. A particular able demagogue or an especially serious mood of national frustration such as that of the Korean War with its help to Joe McC., will increase the ceiling on this Christian army. Tranquility or the availability only of some road company demagogue like Gerald Smith will reduce the numbers. But this fringe is an inescapable aspect of our polity. The singular feature of liberals is their ability to become aroused over each new threat as though it were the first. Perhaps this is good for it becomes the countervailing force. In my view, however, the Birchers, being rather more improbable than most reactionary rally points of recent times, should perhaps be kept and encouraged.

I am going to see Nehru in the next day or two and will perhaps have some comments on how he enjoyed his visit.[89] I have told Desai that while everybody says these visits are a great success they should not be carried away. I said I thought Nehru's visit left you and Washington with the feeling that the Indians were rather irresponsible in their view of events in Southeast Asia and elsewhere. He protested strongly that this was not intended and in nowise the case, but I think it well to have some worry on the point.

Incidentally, the visit was an enormous success from my point of view. I vastly enjoyed the visit to Newport, hearing you for the first time on foreign policy and, most of all, the highly agreeable parties in the White House. As I have written Jackie, the latter were exceptionally enjoyable after the austerity of the New Delhi society and prepare me for a winter of fruit juice receptions, curry, and intense conversations on the political prospects of Mr. Krishna Menon.

I have been dictating this in the plane coming back from Mysore where I have been getting an honorary degree. My rule on these used to be to have one more than Schlesinger.[90] However, I am here caught up in an uncontrollable flood of academic distinction.

> Yours faithfully,
> John Kenneth Galbraith

SECRET

Dear Mr. President:

I think the rearrangement of Mrs. Kennedy's schedule has gone fairly smoothly.[92] There has been a little pettish comment and of course disappointment in the South and Calcutta. Americans are supposed always to confine themselves to the Ganges plain and thus they never see the most attractive part of India. But certainly she can count on a warm and agreeable welcome. Nehru, who is deeply in love and has a picture of himself strolling with JBK displayed all by itself in the main entrance hall of his house, was entirely agreeable. Do tell Jackie that she could have no disorder better calculated to arouse my sympathy than a sinus infection. It still knocks me out at about the same intervals that alcohol used to level my Uncle John and in much the same way.

The tone of Indian-American relations, as viewed from here at least, has improved a lot in the last few weeks. Apart from any beneficial effect from my absence, they have now got over their guilt about Goa,[93] some of which they were taking out on us. And Krishna Menon has been out of town getting reelected. There was never any doubt, incidentally, about his reelection. The only two political organizations in his district are the Congress and the Communists and he had the support of both.

When I am not worrying about your wife, I worry about Indo-China. (Ross once told Thurber in 1940 when he was losing his eyesight: "Thurber, I worry about you and England!")[94] I had a long talk with Felt[95] in Hawaii and have been over the papers and documents again. I continue to be sadly out of step with the Establishment. I can't think Diem has made any significant effort to improve his government either politically or administratively or will. We are increasingly replacing the French as the colonial military force and we will increasingly arouse the resentments associated therewith. Moreover, while I don't think the Russians are clever enough to fix it that way, we are surely playing their game. They couldn't be more pleased than to have us spend our billions in these distant jungles where it does us no good and them no harm.

Incidentally, who is the man in your administration who decides what countries are strategic? I would like to have his name and address and ask him what is so important about this real estate in the space age. What strength do we gain from alliance with an incompetent government and a people who are so largely indifferent to their own salvation. Some of his decisions puzzle me.

But it is the political poison that is really at issue. The Korean war killed us in the early 50's; this involvement could kill us now. That is what the military and the Department will never see. But I must learn to be easier on the State Department. It has a sense of tradition. It believes that because we had a poor foreign policy under Truman and Eisenhower we should have a poor one under Kennedy. No one can complain about that.

There is one ray of light. I think that Hanoi may now be getting worried. The Indians keep saying this—that the North Vietnamese feel they will lose their independence either to the Americans or to the Chinese defending them against the Americans but that in any case they will lose. However this may be, and knowing your distaste for diagnosis without remedy, let me lay down four rules that should govern our policy in this part of the world. They are:

1. Keep up the threshold against the commitment of American combat forces. This is of the utmost importance—a few will mean more and more and more. And then the South Vietnamese boys will go back to the farms. We will do the fighting.

2. Keep civilian control in Saigon. Once the military take over we will have no possibility of working out a disentanglement. I have been disturbed, incidentally, by indications that Harkins[96] might have a standing more or less independent of the Ambassador. That was what cost us so heavily in Korea. Without Brown[97] as boss we would have had no chance of working our way out of Laos.

3. We must keep the door wide open for any kind of a political settlement. In particular we must keep communications open by way of the Indians and even the Russians to Hanoi. If they give any indication of willingness to settle, we should jump at the chance. Any form of disentanglement is going to bring criticism from fighting Joe Alsop[98] as it has in Laos. But the one thing that will cause worse damage and more penetrating attack will be increasing involvement. Politics is not the art of the possible. It consists in choosing between the disastrous and the unpalatable. I wonder if those who talk of a ten-year war really know what they are saying

in terms of American attitudes. We are not as forgiving as the French.

4. Finally, I hold to the view, whatever our public expressions, that any alternative to Diem is bound to be an improvement. I think I mentioned once before that no one ever sees an alternative to the man in power. But when the man in power is on the way down, anything is better.

Yours faithfully,
John Kenneth Galbraith

April 5, 1962[99]

Dear Mr. President:

I have put in a lot of time the last three or four days on the scene of my well-known guerrilla activities, namely, South Vietnam. This included a long and most reassuring discussion with Bob McNamara.[100] We are in basic agreement on most matters and for the rest I think Bob appreciated having some arguments from my side of the fence. I also had two or three long discussions with Averell[101] and the attached memorandum, which is of no breathtaking novelty, comes close to reflecting our combined views. I think I can safely spare you another eloquent restatement of what you have already heard from me several times before. However, I do pray that in addition to reading the attached memorandum you see Governor Harriman at some early date.

I am leaving this afternoon for New York and tomorrow night for India. There are no pressing Indian issues I need to cover with you. Kashmir will continue to simmer.[102] This is not the time for any brilliant initiatives and the best we can do is to press both sides to keep their behavior in low key and keep above the obscene politics ourselves. As I told you attitudes on the Hill toward India seem mellower than I had expected. I am coming back on a very brief private trip in early June to get an honorary degree and make a speech. I will try and give A.I.D.[103] and India a lift before the Senate if, as Fulbright and some others believe it may then be needed.

Last, but not least, I must tell you how much I enjoyed the other evening at Glen Ora,[104] our survey of the problems of the nation and the world, and the chance to reflect on the unique capacity of your advisers to solve them.

Affectionately,
John Kenneth Galbraith

April 4, 1962[105]

Memorandum for the President
Subject: Vietnam

The following considerations influence our thinking on Vietnam:

1. We have a growing military commitment. This could expand step by step into a major, long drawn-out, indecisive military involvement.

2. We are backing a weak and, on the record, ineffectual government and a leader who as a politician may be beyond the point of no return.

3. There is consequent danger we shall replace the French as the colonial force in the area and bleed as the French did.

4. The political effects of some of the measures which pacification requires, or is believed to require, including the concentration of population, relocation of villages, and the burning of old villages, may be damaging to those and especially to Westerners associated with it.

5. We fear that at some point in the involvement there will be a major political outburst about the new Korea and the new war into which the Democrats as so often before have precipitated us.

6. It seems at least possible that the Soviets are not particularly desirous of trouble in this part of the world and that our military reaction with the need to fall back on Chinese protection may be causing concern in Hanoi.

In the light of the foregoing we urge the following:

1. That it be our policy to keep open the door for political solution. We should welcome as a solution any broadly based non-Communist government that is free from external interference. It

should have the requisites for internal law and order. We should not require that it be militarily identified with the United States.

2. We shall find it useful in achieving this result if we seize any good opportunity to involve other countries and world opinion in settlement and its guarantee. This is a useful exposure and pressure on the Communist bloc countries and a useful antidote for the argument that this is a private American military adventure.

3. We should measurably reduce our commitment to the particular leadership of the government of South Vietnam.

To accomplish the foregoing, we recommend the following specific steps:

1. In the next fortnight or so the I.C.C.[106] will present a report which we are confidentially advised will accuse North Vietnam of subversion and the Government of Vietnam in conjunction with the United States of not notifying the introduction of men and material as prescribed by the Geneva Accords. We should respond by asking the co-chairmen to initiate steps to re-establish compliance with the Geneva Accords. Pending specific recommendations, which might at some stage include a conference of signatories, we should demand a suspension of Vietcong activity and agree to a standstill on an introduction of men and material.

2. Additionally, Governor Harriman should be instructed to approach the Russians to express our concern about the increasingly dangerous situation that the Vietcong is forcing in Southeast Asia. They should be told of our determination not to let the Vietcong overthrow the present government while at the same time to look without relish on the dangers that this military build-up is causing in the area. The Soviets should be asked to ascertain whether Hanoi can and will call off the Vietcong activity in return for phased American withdrawal, liberalization in the trade relations between the two parts of the country and general and non-specific agreement to talk about reunification after some period of tranquility.

3. Alternatively, the Indians should be asked to make such an approach to Hanoi under the same terms of reference.

4. It must be recognized that our long-run position cannot involve an unconditional commitment to Diem. Our support is to non-Communist and progressively democratic government not to individuals. We cannot ourselves replace Diem. But we should be

clear in our mind that almost any non-Communist change would probably be beneficial and this should be the guiding rule for our diplomatic representation in the area.

In the meantime policy should *continue* to be guided by the following:

1. We should resist all steps which commit American troops to combat action and impress upon all concerned the importance of keeping American forces out of actual combat commitment.

2. We should disassociate ourselves from action, however necessary, which seems to be directed at the villagers, such as the new concentration program. If the action is one that is peculiarly identified with Americans, such as defoliation, it should not be undertaken in the absence of most compelling reasons. Americans in their various roles should be as invisible as the situation permits.

Bombay, India
May 7, 1962

CONFIDENTIAL
ITS-10[107]

Dear Mr. President:

It is some time since you have had one of these reports, a gap to be related more or less equally to the state of my stomach,[108] the pressure of other tasks including most recently the need to complete some travel before the heat here becomes unbearable, and the absence of any information for which, by my best assessment, you could have an uncontrollable thirst.

I am writing from Bombay where I have just spent an hour or two with your Secretary of State.[109] We had a useful and agreeable session. While I still do not find him the easy, confident, forthcoming, eclectic and commanding figure with which in my imagination I associate the diplomacy of the New Frontier, we get along much better than hitherto. This is partly because, in some indefinable way, our foreign policy does seem to me to show increasing evidence of thought. But as you are aware I grow mellower by the month.

My most recent major worry has been over testing and the danger of a major anti-American explosion with some serious effect on fundamental public and political attitudes.[110] However, we have come through all right. We are getting only a few strictly CP demonstrations. The press, politicians and public are not aroused even in this congenial environment. Partly it is the general good management by the Kennedy Administration. We have managed to establish our reputation for good sense and restraint; we obviously responded to the Soviet initiative with reluctance; we have managed to keep in focus the simple fact that the Russians did it first.

I suspect also that this is the reward for a lot of patient and tedious effort. Clearly the government, press, students and pundits do not want to embarrass us on the issue. And one reason is that our cultivation of the universities and press, your unrewarding hours with Nehru last autumn, Jackie's visit and other efforts have persuaded the Indians that we are good people and they have no righteous obligation to embarrass us.

Incidentally, I hope the series will be run as rapidly through to conclusion as possible. Time deepens the effect and engages passions. I also strongly endorse the policy of the minimum of needful publicity and avoidance of comment on the destructive virtuosity of the gadgets we are testing.

One of my current problems is Ayub's[111] compulsively repeated statements that he will use American arms against India if the need arise. He said it again last week and, naturally, the Indian press reacted joyously. It greatly helps those who want to buy Soviet aircraft, an enterprise I am trying to stand off. There was never such a drastic misadventure in modern diplomacy as these minor alliances of Dulles. Machiavelli warned weak princes against joining with a strong one. In my forthcoming revision of his work I will warn all strong states against weak sisters. Since weak states are weak, the strong state gets no added strength out of its alliance. (That is axiomatic though I am aware of the electronic exceptions in the era of modern technology.) But the weak state can use its stronger ally for its own purposes. Since the state is small and weak, its purposes will be small and undignified. To these the large state becomes a party and such is our present fate. From the Portuguese to General Phoumi[112] our indigent allies are principally concerned with how to use the U.S. to promote their puny affairs.

In fact the United States should stand in majesty and grandeur above such matters. Involved we lose our influence. Above we could have great influence. The major NATO powers apart, I cannot think of anything so important as that we have a gradual but inflexible will to remove ourselves from special relationships with the Albanias of the world and be prepared, instead, to help and treat all alike. There is of course nothing in the experience of being Ambassador to India which argues against this view. But this was always our instinct and it shouldn't surprise us that we were right.

One feature of the State Department mind on which I find I have not mellowed is its profound moral conviction that established policy is to be preferred to the one that is best for the United States.

I am coming back more or less privately for a few days in early June to get an honorary degree and possibly get some more of the medical advice for which I am becoming a kind of global customer. I plan in a speech to develop the point you raised at Glen Ora; namely, what, on candid view, are the advantages and disadvantages of communism as compared with our mixture from the viewpoint of the new and developing country. Thought, as distinct from *obiter dicta,* will show I think that we do have some important advantages and, more than incidentally, that we have some faults that if remedied would add to our margin of advantage. In accordance with established procedures, I will send you a copy.

My recent travels have taken me up along the Chinese frontier and back to the Burma border. (In some of these places they hadn't even heard of Bowles.) In addition to their better-publicized problems with the Chinese, the Indians are having very serious trouble in living with people within their own borders. This is an area with a large number of ethnically separate groups and all are unhappy in their present relations with the Indians. The Nagas are in open revolt and tie down a couple of divisions but they are only the extreme case.[113] A half dozen other ethnic or linguistic groups are asking what they can have in the way of independence, autonomy or self-determination. It is an interesting place to study the problems of neocolonialism.[114]

Yours faithfully,
John Kenneth Galbraith

June 6, 1962

Memorandum for the President

In the last month or so newspaper stories—most of them emanating from David Lawrence's center for political incantation[115]—have announced my unsettlement and candidacy for other callings. I had given this little thought until JBK told me the other evening that you thought I might be restless. The following, to the best of my knowledge and introspection, are the facts.

(1) I expect I can do you more good in India than elsewhere. I would like to make my stay there a complete and workmanlike chapter in my life and that of the Administration.

(2) When that is done I would like to return to writing which is the major support to my vanity. As I think you know, I am not fond of the Washington mass.

(3) I am not restless. I retain my concern for the domestic economic and international problems with which you struggle, but there is a difference here between concern and any yearning for command.

(4) On occasion during these past months I have been a trifle discouraged about my health. It seems clear that there is nothing organically amiss so I have hopes of becoming better accommodated to climate, routine or whatever is causing the trouble.

J. K. Galbraith

New Delhi, India
July 13, 1962[116]

Dear Mr. President:

Carl has sent me a letter with a penetrating item by Ruth Montgomery which could lead me to hope that you might cut off the *Journal American* too.[117] However, my further thought is that perhaps I should give you a succinct view of exactly what I am doing here. I sense a remote but discouraging tendency for you to imagine (a) that I have become a financial arm of the Indian Government; (b) that my task is to defend the Indians to the United States; (c) that I yearn to be loved. None, not even the last, reflects in fact my preoccupation. In fact, I find Indian politics depressing and not less so on continued contact. The thought crosses my mind more often than you might think as to why Galbraith cultivates this particular vineyard. I also spend my time trying to persuade the Indians of our problems and point of view but, since I need no particular help in this, it is not in my recurrent advice to the State Department. Here is what concerns me:

India is a peasant and bourgeois, property-owning and, in the aggregate, conservative community. It is held to the West by ties of language and tradition of considerable strength. Most of the effective political leaders are on our side—a distinct oddity as the world goes. Their position depends on their history in the independence movement, the inherent conservatism of the country, the fact that our food eliminates the desperation that would result from hunger, and because planning plus our aid gives a semblance of progress.

Working against these conservative influences is a combination of the Communist, the angry, the frustrated, the xenophobic, and the anti-Moslem. Increasingly in recent years, and rapidly in recent months they have been coalescing around Menon. And Menon with great brilliance has made himself the custodian of the particular inflammatory issues—Goa, arms aid to Pakistan, Kashmir[118]— which put us automatically on the other side.

A disaster in this part of the world, as I see it, would be considerably worse not only for the United States but for the political reputation of the New Frontier than a disaster in Indo-China. Accordingly, as your man hereabouts, I assume I should seek to prevent it. Aid is a substantial part of my armory and that is my interest. I don't exclude a certain compassion for poor people. If one lacked compassion he would not see the full importance of our assistance.

I am equally concerned to arrest the impulse of the State Department and my old friend Adlai Stevenson to show mighty indignation on irrelevant issues. That is why I was so anxious to cut our losses on Portuguese colonialism. It is why we simply cannot have another debate on Kashmir and State must be prevented from drifting on in to it. It is also why our arms aid to Pakistan is a two-edged sword that cuts principally on the wrong side.

Yours faithfully,
John Kenneth Galbraith

New Delhi, India
August 6, 1962

Dear Mr. President:

I learn in the newspapers of your long summer evenings in the White House and it occurs to me that I should help you out with some good reading.

Politically things remain in a repulsive state. Nehru is still in indifferent health although he has picked up strength during the last few weeks while parliament has been in recess. (It assembles again today.) For years the reins have been nearly all in his hands. Now he neither drives nor relinquishes. The other ministers, with the exception of Menon—and to some extent Desai[119]—are so completely accustomed to passivity that they cannot change.

Menon continues his drive and, I am sure, has considerable plans for an autumn campaign in New York and perhaps elsewhere. He got a large boost out of the Kashmir debate[120] and has certainly considered ways and means of getting another lift including the possibility of some shooting along the Pakistan border. This would also have the merit of taking attention away from China where his sympathies and fellow-travelling instincts make him vulnerable. (He is also I think worrying considerably lest the China border flareup[121] give the Soviets second thoughts on MIG's[122] with the slap at China thus implied.) The snow closes off any danger from the Chinese around the middle of November. Until then last year the Chinese had been dominating the headlines; Menon completely cured that by going into Goa.[123] I would be surprised if the notion of a repeat performance has entirely escaped him. However there are also more risks this time.

I continue to feel fairly clear on the policy we should follow which involves a careful triangulation between Menon and his supporters, his opposition here and your opposition in Washington. We must do everything possible to avoid building Menon up as we have in the past. This includes, to replay a record, denying him the highly emotional issues at the UN and concerning Pakistan that we have given him in the past and making it clear that we consider him a kind of antique radical whose tactic of alienating everyone in sight is a diplomatic novelty that does more harm to India than anyone else. In a curious way he is the Hindu Dulles—alienating people as he goes. (Give the phrase Hindu Dulles to someone.)

For Menon's opponents our basic policy is the aid program. It makes them the responsible people who hold the country together.

I am also persuaded that it would have a good effect here and a good ultimate effect in Washington if we were to be cooler in our general technical, economic and cultural assistance to India than in the past and I have been moving along this line. In past years we have sometimes been so eager to help and so anxious to explain ourselves that the Indians have forgotten both how to ask or be grateful and they have come to conclude that it is the business of the world to understand *them*. Even our friends do not get credit for help that is too eagerly offered—and which the opposition hastens to say the Americans will provide anyway.

I have been making it clear that I think the Indian reaction to our problems in getting them aid is exceedingly curious. I am taking up the subject in suitably broad, bland terms in a speech to Indian M.P.'s this week.

Some of this bears on my own role here. Our original conception of Indian policy now going on two years ago was that by aid and the right kind of representation we could get considerable help from the Indians. We haven't got much and I doubt that my high-minded salesmanship of the New Frontier has been at fault. I am enormously admired up to the very moment when I make a request. I will go into my future, a topic which crosses even my totally selfless mind, sometime in the future.

As you will have seen, I have put the MIG discussion on ice. I think it served a useful purpose. We raised the threshold against buying Soviet equipment and we let our friends in the Armed Services here know there was an alternative. However I must say that Menon, with his control of all channels of technical knowledge, shot down the Lightning[124] with appalling ease. In the end I began to develop a few reservations, which I gather you shared, about the cost (in overseas dollars) of this package.

I am still far from certain that the MIG deal is going to come off. I have been spreading the idea that they are useless toys with some success, and I continue to think that the Soviets will be reluctant to arouse Chinese passions at a time when they are pressing the Chinese and Indians to stop playing war with their elbows on the northern border.

I gather your interest, unlike mine, still turns to the domestic American scene. I can see nothing from here in the last two months that causes me to regret my advice on taxes. It looks simple to raise and lower taxes. That is the mistake of economists. For considering the political and constitutional history and lore in which they are embedded they are, in fact, the most rigid of instruments of economic control.

I notice also that the Gallup poll plus the grass roots researches of Fuller Brush Alsop[125] confirm my feeling that the people are still not acculturated to tax manipulation. This is not a decisive point. They weren't ready for spending under Roosevelt either. Still it suggests that spending is the more conservative and acceptable course.

All of this leads me to hope that the CEA and the Bureau of the Budget are being pressed to get ready a really wide-ranging expenditure program for the new year. It may not be easier to change taxes then. And the economy might need a boost.

Is the space program getting all the money that it can use? It seems to have a considerable capacity to absorb dollars and I gather it is one of those things that the Congress regards with affection. I must say I also find the whole thing enormously exciting.

Yours faithfully,
John Kenneth Galbraith

New Delhi, India
August 31, 1962

Dear Mr. President:

I have just been reading the transcript of your press conference yesterday. I must say I have the most complete admiration for these performances and, more than incidentally, of the preparation that so obviously goes into them.

I was struck again at how reactionary and slanted many of the press questions are. It is extraordinary how many reflect Dulles's attitude on foreign policy to the extent that they are not those of Major-General Edwin A. Walker.[126] However, I think that your calm reactions reflect the mood of the American people. Our first thoughts are always bellicose. But then, as Bury[127] says of the Athenians, reason intervenes.

Things continue quiet here, although I suppose Menon has some unpleasantness in mind. The papers here gave big and favorable play to your press conference comment on MIG's[128] and have been full of speculation about the letter Nehru sent to you. As you perhaps may have guessed, I was aware of the latter. It is important that the Indians develop a sense of obligation on these matters. One way of insuring that they do is to have them express it. I have kept knowledge of my role quiet.

I grow a little alarmed at the ease with which I am learning to suffer the State Department. I accept with complete equanimity things that a year ago I considered impossible. The trouble is not that the Department is conservative or wrong-headed. Rather it is totally committed to a kind of officious dullness. Anything that involves the slightest imagination or even brightness of mind is a departure from policy. You see the top. The bottom is often worse.

Yours faithfully,
John Kenneth Galbraith

New Delhi, India
October 16, 1962[129]

Dear Mr. President:

I remember when I was running price control the only news ever passed up to me was of major disasters. The intelligence reaching your office must be much the same. In recent weeks things here have been going sufficiently better so that it requires a major act of will to talk about them. However, perhaps you need a moment's relaxation.

The political situation is much improved. The Chinese have had a disastrous effect on Krishna.[130] Deep in his heart, poor man, he feels that we are the real enemies with the Pakistanis in second place. But the Chinese have come over the hill and he cannot ignore them. Evidently he had a very bad conscience about going to the UN and he has now postponed a return trip. Yesterday in a speech in Bangalore he pleaded with everyone not to become too excited about the Chinese and tried to get his other enemies back in the picture. The wail was audible. The problem, as perhaps I have said before, is much like that of the British communist after the Ribbentrop-Molotov pact or an American fellow traveller during the Korean War. He is whipsawed between his political faith and the pressures of nationalism.

The Prime Minister seems to be in better health and much improved in morale.

My policy on the border conflict, in the convenient absence of instructions, is to express quiet sympathy, make clear that we hope for settlement here as elsewhere, and not to feel any urgency about offering help. It will be far better if the Indians have to ask. They must not think we are yearning for an opportunity to line them up on our side and save them.

I have just completed an interesting and rather encouraging experiment. I took some twenty or thirty Indian newspapermen and photographers plus two American television crews and a newsreel crew on a ten-day tour of American-aided projects in India. We travelled by special train—a delight in itself and, I hasten to say, at no expense either to balance of payments or the United States taxpayer. (We have enough rupees available for United States use to last well into John Jr.'s second term.) Apart from a major University speech at Lucknow, another center of antipathetic attitudes toward the United States, the hegira included (by way of illustration) the new Indian Institute of Technology at Kanpur, support for which we announced a year ago; several power plants which we are financing; two coal washeries, which may well be the least fascinating industrial processes in the world; a huge dam near Hyderabad which is being financed by Public Law 480 rupees on which 100,000 people (sic) are employed; all kinds of agricultural betterment; a big fertilizer plant; an automobile and truck plant; a school for training mechanics and draftsmen and two schools for the training of young workers in the operation and care of bulldozers, steam shovels and the like.

Everywhere there was a lively appreciation of the source of the aid. Invariably there was a sign saying it was being done with the cooperation of the United States. And there was a good deal of enthusiasm on the part of those who were on the payroll. The tour got a great deal of national attention and it blanketed the local papers. I held a more or less continuous seminar on economic development which must have been highly rewarding to all listeners.

Many things about A.I.D.[131] still worry me. While I have been trying to do fewer things and making sure that these are the most important, there is still room for further concentration. We still need to move more of our people out of Delhi—it is like pulling teeth to accomplish this. Some very odd people get recruited. The Indian industrial management is highly bureaucratic—at a big fertilizer plant outside Bombay they had—characteristically—put up a vast office building before they had started excavations for the plant itself. Still there is much that is good. A lot of the projects selected by my predecessors were exceedingly sound and the program could easily suffer from too much reform. Out in Kotah (a Godforsaken desert community in Rajasthan)[132] I encountered a Californian by the name of Childs married to a Japanese wife who for four years has been the only American in town. He has done a superb job of organizing a school for training in the operation and maintenance of bulldozers, graders, heavy trucks and so forth and is just about ready to turn it over to Indian direction. There are many other such cases.

I have been following the aid legislation in the Congress this year with a good deal of misgiving. I would gather there is even more serious trouble ahead in the future. I have a suggestion for giving it a new lift which I will put to you when I am back—that is, if I can catch you for a few minutes between whistle stops. I am in Washington week after next—October 30 to November 6.

Is Cuba worse than the bomb shelter eruption of a year ago?[133] The Mississippi affair seemed from here to have been superbly handled.[134] Without question it greatly raised our stock in this part of the world. Not even the Communists now seriously accuse us of evasion.

> Yours faithfully,
> John Kenneth Galbraith

Telegram
CONFIDENTIAL

Knowing your preoccupations,[135] I have tried to keep local war off your hands.[136] Moreover our course and decisions which I have been reporting have seemed fairly clear. However as you will have sensed, things have been moving at a very rapid pace here and I now foresee the need for a major political decision in the next couple of days on which I need your judgment as well as frank protection.[137]

We are now certain to be asked for military assistance in considerable volume. This involves no immediate response and, indeed, we should show ourselves to be deliberate on the matter. (I have no doubt in the end that we must help.) We must also make clear, as I have already started doing, that any help will require Indians, in their own interest, to be more considerate of our political and public opinion than in recent past. However, the immediate question concerns Menon . . . [material censored]. Menon has supporters and a loud press. Against this is the favorable effect on American public opinion and on our ability to work with Indians and prospect of strengthening administration hand in dealing with public and Congress on behalf of India. I especially need your assessment of latter prospect. You will sense that this is a matter for more than routine guidance.

Telegram

If, as today's news suggests, the Cuban crisis is easing could I beg your assistance on some of my urgent requests of recent days. Our affairs here are, I believe, well in hand but the absence of communication naturally stirs misgiving especially in light of my tendency to assume inadequacy unless opposite proved. I need especially to know if importance of impressing Pakistanis of seriousness of Communist threat is fully realized in Washington. This needs to be done at highest and firmest level. Can I also be clear that as and when we are asked for arms their parochial objections will not be a factor for this would be fatal. For peace of mind I would appreciate assurance as soon as possible of contingency planning on lines of Embtel 1384 and nature of thinking and needs. Large forces are involved, and our minds must be open to worst. I want to be sure calmness is not being equated with equanimity. I am also keenly anxious for president's view on strategy re Menon. Finally to alleviate my sense of total outrage do note my telegram 1373 and Deptel 1651 in reply. The McMahon line which relates to NEFA and does not involve Pakistan is indeed sanctioned by all recent usage. What a hell of a time to have to start a study.[138] Important things are at stake and one cannot be pecked to death by ducks.

New Delhi, India
November 13, 1962[139]

Dear Mr. President:

I have been wanting for the past ten days to give you a more detailed and intimate account of our affairs here. I have been sending rather full dispatches to the Department, some of which you have doubtless seen. But as you will have discovered, few Ambassadors have ever been completely candid in such reporting. There is truth and there is also what one must have believed. I merely try to minimize the difference.

These past three weeks have brought great change here—no doubt the greatest change in public attitudes since World War II. The most treasured of preconceptions have been shattered. The disillusion with the Chinese is of course total. So, save at the top, is that with the Soviets. And the other unaligneds are not very popular. Nehru remains an exception. Even he is now hoping only for friendly neutrality from the Soviets rather than active support. But with him there is another factor. All his life he has sought to avoid being dependent upon the United States and the United Kingdom— most of his personal reluctance to ask (or thank) for aid has been based on this pride. He did not like it because it advertised what hurt his pride. Now nothing is so important to him, more personally than politically, than to maintain the semblance of this independence. His age no longer allows of readjustment. To a point we can, I feel, be generous on this.[140]

One thing much on my mind these last days has been the American press. We have had a great influx of correspondents plus a large itinerant delegation covering the arms lift. . . . Were they bottled up here, the Indians would get a bad press and so, *inter alia,* would we. I have now pretty well broken through on this, though I had to go to the Prime Minister himself. There will be many stories on the infirm character of his leadership, but that is not our business. I think Nehru is still playing down our role to protect the sensitivities of the Soviets and perhaps, more especially, to protect his own feelings. I have told him this was something we couldn't take and have pictured the repercussions in the American press. We cannot decently help someone who is afraid to be seen in our company. There will be some damage along these lines, I fear.

The great question is what the Chinese intend. In the beginning I thought that this was essentially a border conflict. The Chinese have a serious claim to the Aksai Chin Plateau in Ladakh. It provides them with a strategic access to Sinkiang and they had been building their road there for two years before the Indians reacted. By getting a good foothold in the east, they could establish a claim for the area they really want. In addition, no doubt, they are motivated by jealousy and dislike plus the feeling that Indians are the world's safest object of animosity. So with their superior ready manpower and equipment they could show the Indians and the Asian countries that in military affairs at least they had superiority. All this could be accomplished by a major border demonstration. I have not entirely discarded the above theory. But last week the trickle of evidence on forces north of the frontier, the concentration in the real danger areas which are the Chumbi Valley and back near the Burma border, the incursions and patrol actions in new places and the drift of Chinese propaganda caused me to conclude that we should assume something more serious. The Indians have consistently underestimated Chinese intentions. In one way or another our estimate influences them. And, of course, we are in less danger if we have to withdraw from a too somber estimate than if we must revise a too sanguine one. In the former instance we shall have at least done some of the right things. My recent estimates have reflected the above considerations. Deep in my own mind I am not persuaded that the Chinese are as ambitious as this implies or that they can be so indifferent to the deterrent effects of our position.

If the Chinese should really come down the mountain in force, there will be more political changes here. Much so-called nonalignment [has already gone] out the window. . . . Popular opinion and our military assistance [have] worked a further and major impairment. The problem in face of a really serious attack would be how we would react to the prospect of a new, large and extremely expensive ally. I personally hope the Chinese do not force this choice.[141] The Indians are busy worrying about the end of nonalignment. It is we that should be doing the worrying on this.

Generally speaking, I think our affairs here are in good shape. We have managed to appear as a solid and steadfast friend.[142] Even the left press has not seriously pinned on us the charge that we are seeking to entangle or otherwise exploit the situation. On most matters our course has seemed clear. During the Cuban affair I moved ahead but with a fairly good sense of what would be in your mind. The period has not been without interest.

We do have a serious problem next door and this has been much on my mind. The Pakistanis have not taken the attack very seriously and have seen it as the great opportunity to get concessions from the Indians. As I am sure Ayub[143] himself saw, no one could press the Indians in their moment of despair. But instead the Pakistanis were pressed themselves for assurances. And our weapons, in an action not too gracefully cleared with the Pakistanis, started coming to India. Their disappointment is understandable. I have worked hard and I think with a certain measure of success here. The Ministry of External Affairs at my behest has asked the press to be very quiet in response to the Pakistan fulminations. I have given strong encouragement to a Congress Party group which is urging reconciliation with Pakistan. I have pressed the Indians to give the Pakistanis information on Indian troop movements and I succeeded last week in getting Nehru to write a long and friendly letter to Ayub on the situation, while their new High Commissioner is proposing the resumption of ministerial talks. Meanwhile McConaughy[144] has been doing noble work in Karachi to calm the Pakistanis and make them see that the threat is to the subcontinent. My sense of the situation is that we should not press the Pakistanis any more in the immediate future. However I should continue all moderating efforts here. Eventually but not too soon the Indians must be asked to propose meaningful negotiations on Kashmir.[145] This should not, incidentally, raise the question of a plebiscite, an idea in which there is no longer any future. The only hope lies in having a full guarantee of the headwaters of the rivers. Each side should hold on to the mountain territory that it has and there should be some sort of shared responsibility for the Valley. I really don't think that a solution on these lines is impossible. It may be wise incidentally when the time comes to have the British do it as a Commonwealth exercise.

With the great advantage of perspective, I regard the election results as a strong endorsement of the Kennedy Administration, your Cuban policy and the persistence of Mr. Endicott Peabody.[146]

Yours faithfully,
John Kenneth Galbraith

New Delhi, India
December 6, 1962[147]

Dear Mr. President:

I think I should give you a somewhat more intimate view of developments here than you will be getting from the cables. I assume that you are probably suffering from a considerable surfeit of information on India at the moment—that you are hearing more about penguins than you need to know. However, the changes here continue to be great.

On the military side I am just back from a two-day tour of the front. I went up to the forward positions to look things over for myself. As on all things having to do with the military, it is a great deal better to be observant and intelligent than to be professional if you can't be both. The Indian Army has now recovered its balance, morale is improving, the soldiers are rough, hard and well-trained and discipline is good. Nevertheless, it is well that the Chinese stopped. While there was (and is) no question of their invading the Ganges Plain, they could do a great deal of damage if they decided to come on again. That is because the Indian Army in its command, organization, tactics and equipment is extremely old-fashioned. The individual soldiers carry personal arms that are sixty years old and this can hardly give them the feeling of equality with opponents carrying modern light automatic weapons. The tactics are stuffy and rigid. Success depends to a considerable extent on the hope that the Chinese will reform and fight on the roads like Germans and not bypass fixed defenses. I visited one unit north of Tezpur which was admirably placed and dug in. It would give the Chinese a very bad time if they came that way. When I asked the C-in-C what would prevent the Chinese from giving it a miss right or left, he said "nothing." On these plains they should have a great advantage over lightly armed Chinese with their armor. Unfortunately, the latter is antique, starved for parts and cannot be easily deployed because of poor bridges.

Some of the commanders are very good. More are still the amiable frauds that rise to the top in any peacetime Army. Fortunately, I think they have one of their best commanders in the area of greatest danger—the so-called Siliguri Gap below the Chumbi Valley in Tibet. This is the most accessible route into India from China and the one that could most easily cut off Eastern India and threaten East Pakistan. I am sure we were right to urge them to use the ceasefire to play for time.

However, while I assume that the Chinese have not given up their evil intentions, my instinct is that the danger of a new and major adventure is receding. They have dealt India a very heavy blow, which is certainly one thing they had in mind. They have also established a strong position for bargaining in Ladakh. And I am inclined to think they took Nehru's talk about nonalignment seriously and were honestly surprised at the speed with which we reacted. If they move again, they must wonder what they will provoke and what will happen to their very long supply lines.

So the immediate military phase may well be over. The Indians will be very cautious in their reaction while continuing to make clear that their long-run intentions toward the Chinese are exceedingly lethal. This is probably the right policy. Nehru would be thrown out if we made peace even on fairly favorable terms. But they are in no position to make war. This brings me to the political situation, which is exceedingly interesting.

The Chinese cost Menon his job.[148] But they have also driven a considerable wedge between Nehru and the people. By strongly coming to India's support, but at the same time giving no grounds for suspicion of ulterior motives, there has been a simply enormous enhancement of American prestige. The press, Army, politicians, indeed the country as a whole, has come almost overnight to regard us as a first friend. As I predicted, even the word nonalignment has disappeared from everything but Nehru's speeches and the left-wing press, and there is a lively discussion as to whether we will insist on it. U.S.I.S. has for years conducted a poll on attitudes toward the United States. In October, 1957, 2.5 percent reported a "Very Good" opinion of the United States. In mid-October, 1962, it was 7.0 percent. Last week it was 62 percent. Eighty-five percent of those asked reported an improved view of the United States.

Less distinctly, there is a great desire for some kind of reconciliation with Pakistan. This has survived all of the loud and angry misbehavior of the Pakistan press and politicians these last weeks. Popular opinion would reject any outright ceding of the Valley. But it is well ahead of Nehru in the desire for some other form of settlement and with the ceasefire many feel that concessions can now be made without indication of weakness. . . .

However, if we handle ourselves with intelligence, we can deal with the situation. We must work with Nehru in spite of his present mood. Any punitive tendency could consolidate and alienate the very great forces that are still on his side. We must avoid this and meanwhile let public opinion work on him. This means in practical terms that we must be responsive to their defense needs and thus to their major source of anxiety. When the Chinese subside we will want to take a good look at the more Napoleonic plans of the Indians for defense. It would be fatal, however, to show hesitancy at this moment when they are relying on us and when the fear of the Chinese is so great. Now that we have got the Kashmir issue out in the open—a significant achievement in itself—we must press it but in such a manner as not to involve ourselves in the inbuilt antagonisms between the two countries. We must continue to make it clear to the Indians that it is their task, not ours and not Pakistan's. In my view, incidentally, Kashmir is not soluble in territorial terms. But by holding up the example of the way in which France and Germany have moved to soften their antagonism by the Common Market and common instruments of administration, including such territorial disputes as that over the Saar, there is a chance of getting the Indo-Pakistan dialogue into constructive channels. . . .

Finally, you will have seen my telegrams on the problem of air defense and the opportunities I see here. In my view it provides a long-run foundation for a political association of the first importance. There are also costs and dangers and I gather that my telegrams are at least producing adequate attention to these. The Department also assures me that you are firmly committed to the notion that the British should look after India in this department. This is perhaps a little like urging that they resume a long-run interest in Ireland. However, I shall postpone discussion of this until I get a full view of what I shall require by way of argument. We can hardly deplore the fact that people have faith in us as they do not in our cousins.

More seriously, I think the liberal West in general and the New Frontier in particular have remarkable opportunities in the realignment that is going on here. It is indeed perhaps the kind of opportunity that comes once in a generation. To seize it involves neither boldness nor caution but only an intelligent reaction to events.

Yours faithfully,
John Kenneth Galbraith

P.S. One problem which I more than slightly fear is this. As the Chinese threat recedes, the communists and fellow-traveling left will try to reassert itself. Their line will be obvious. The Chinese tried to take the mountains in NEFA.[149] However, the Americans in cooperation with the Moslems tried to take our far richer heritage in Kashmir. This could be serious. I have protected this flank by always saying that we aren't urging the surrender of Kashmir or any other particular solution. We are urging the importance of a settlement as a prime goal of Indian foreign policy, for that makes our military aid both possible and effective. I don't think we have run any serious risk here so far. But we must move with care.

New Delhi, India
January 29, 1963

Dear Mr. President:

It is some time since I have written which is the result of a happy coincidence of affairs. There has been very little in the recent handling of matters in Washington which I have felt the need to correct. And things continue here to reveal the inevitable consequences of competence and finesse. When I mention Washington, I must say that I am still not reconciled to tax reduction[150] and I am alarmed at the applause from the wrong people. Still, in accordance with Lenin's principles of democratic centralism, the decision having been taken I am lapsing into silence. Do keep the issue of tax reduction closely tied to reform. Since no one wants the reform, at least to the point of giving up his own loopholes, this will protect you from the reduction. Then you will be under pressure to spend to keep the economy going. And while no one much worries about the economy except your old-fashioned, chart-bitten economists the public will reward you for the things you buy.

The tax reduction issue apart, I thought the State of the Union message very good.[151] Your finest contribution to general enlightenment, however, was the television program in December.[152] I got a print of it here and am showing it to Cabinet Ministers, parliamentarians, press, educators—indeed, to anyone with the outward aspect of solvency, and it is still making the rounds. It has met with universal applause and customers have the added delight of trying to figure out what Sander Vanocur was trying to say.

I see our present job here as involving three fairly straightforward and only mildly self-contradictory tasks. These are:

(1) To keep the Indians firm against the Chinese.
(2) To get a settlement with Pakistan.
(3) To make it clear that we expect their support elsewhere against the Chinese.

I am not absolutely sure of winning on any one but I think all are worth a good try. On the first, I am confident. Public opinion is bitterly anti-Chinese and anticommunist. Nehru himself is reacting to the hostility which the Chinese show to him personally. We can't be entirely sorry for the restraint that he exercises on those who want to launch a five-year war for the liberation of Ladakh and then march on Lhasa.

I have moved members of the Government quite a bit on Pakistan and the drift of public opinion is favorable. I haven't yet made any progress with [Nehru]. He still shows a strong tendency to clam up when I get on to the subject. However, I shall keep on trying.

I gather you have doubts about my third enterprise—that of persuading the Indians that they should share with us the task of containing the Chinese. I still think it a useful exercise. The Chinese are not quarreling with the Soviets over some academic points of doctrine. They are, one must assume, serious about their revolution.

The natural area of expansion is in this part of the world. The only Asian country which really stands in their way is India and *pari passu* the only Western country that is assuming responsibility is the United States. It seems obvious to me there should be some understanding between the two countries. We should expect to make use of India's political position, geographic position, political power and manpower or anyhow ask.

I am opening the new residence this afternoon in considerable style. It is a handsome building, very expensive and highly impractical. I like it very much. I have quietly told all Congressional delegations who have asked about the cost that it was all planned under the previous Administration. I suspect, incidentally, that Republicans are better builders than we are. They are more luxurious in their tastes, more inclined to be lavish with personal perquisites, less concerned to avoid undemocratic ostentation. All this makes for more interesting architecture. Even Hoover and Mellon, miserly though they were on matters of social policy, spent well on public buildings. As a result they did far more for Washington than FDR.

Yours faithfully,
John Kenneth Galbraith

P.S. I have a footnote on the reputation of the New Frontier for race consciousness. I dedicated a collection of essays that I published a couple of years ago to Professor Black[153] and his wife—it read, "To the Blacks." The French translation arrived today. The dedication, in French, reads, "To the Negroes."

New Delhi, India
March 4, 1963

Dear Mr. President:

The local papers came forth with the encouraging news from Washington the other day that in due course I would resign and be replaced by Mr. Chester Bowles. When the local Alsops and Bartletts[154] arrived I confirmed that I would be going back to Harvard in the autumn but maintained a commendable and possibly even unnatural reticence on the subject of my successor.

This is to suggest my own preferences as to timing and those which I would believe reasonably consonant with the situation here and the wishes of my unquestionably very sensible and possibly heat prone successor. Discipline and duty will of course cause me to meet your preference if that be different.

I would like to take some time off in May. After inaugurating a social science center in Japan, having my anatomy examined briefly at Tripler in Hawaii and giving a Charter Day address at the University of California, I plan some holidays in Vermont. This will put me in Washington for the Radhakrishnan[155] visit and back in India sometime in early June. I understand you have a provisional promise to the University of Massachusetts for commencement. I have promised in considerable confidence to back you up in case you cannot make it. All of this assumes the Chinese do not come back which I think is unlikely.

The summer is a very quiet time here and I will cover enough of it so that my successor can arrive when the weather starts to become tolerable in the autumn. Should he like to come earlier and be introduced to New Delhi during the heat and monsoon, that is more than satisfactory to me.

When I see you next, by the way, I want to do some lobbying on behalf of my deputy here this last two years—a Rhodes scholar, a friend of Arthur's and one of the ablest and most energetic men I have ever known. His name is Lane Timmons. He should be made an ambassador somewhere where there is serious work to do.[156]

Yours faithfully,
John Kenneth Galbraith

New Delhi, India
March 5, 1963

Dear Mr. President:

I wonder if you have ever read Thucydides on the Republican reaction to your Cuban policy? Actually he was talking about some tendencies among the Corcyraeans. But one can't be bothered with details. His comment is as follows:

"Impulsive rashness was held the mark of a man, caution in conspiracy was a specious excuse for avoiding action. A violent attitude was always to be trusted, its opponents were suspect. To succeed in a plot was shrewd, it was still more clever to divine one: but if you devised a policy that made such success or suspicion needless, you were breaking up your party and showing fear of your opponents. In fine, men were applauded if they forestalled an injury . . . that had not been conceived."

Yours faithfully,
John Kenneth Galbraith

June 17, 1963

SECRET. Handle via Comint Channels Only [telegram]
To White House
Eyes Only for Bundy and the President from Galbraith

I am reacting to suggestion of Ayub of Eisenhower as a Kashmir mediator because Talbot has been advancing this proposal in Washington and he or someone might take encouragement from the fact that it is now suggested from Karachi. The idea as I indicated to Averell is utterly bad. Were Ike to do it, which I assume is doubtful, it should be a staff job in which he would be a figurehead. This is completely the wrong kind of mediator. The right man is the one who will stay with the job himself over a long period of time and accustom both sides to a reasonable solution. Ike's name has no advantage whatever for neither Ayub nor Nehru is in the slightest measure susceptible to big-name influence. And finally there is possibility Eisenhower would inject a note of partisan politics into the picture which I suspect is what Ayub has in mind. There is already some tendency for the Democrats to be the partisan of India and conservative Republicans the partisan of Pakistan and this tendency should be given no encouragement. If Ike came up with a pro-Pakistan proposal it would be easy and tempting for Republicans by giving all-out support to embarrass administration and damage its India policy.

New Delhi, India
July 9, 1963

CONFIDENTIAL

Dear Mr. President:

This is my last report from this precinct. I haven't flooded you with literature in these last months because there was little that needed to go on your platter. The problems have been manageable.

On the whole, and with some reservations about the future to which I will come presently, things are in good shape. Our prestige is high. The left is in total disorder. Menon is gone, so has Malaviya,[157] his last ally in the Cabinet. Menon's new papers are said to be doing badly. The Soviets continue to give evidence of considerable uncertainty in their Indian policy. I think that by reacting promptly last autumn we insured a considerable measure of future caution on the part of the Chinese. At the same time we have avoided seeming to be belligerent about it. I think I have succeeded in getting our relations with the Indians on to a slightly more self-respecting basis in which we help them without smothering them with kindness and do not hesitate to ask for what we want in return. However, some improvement in this latter department is still possible. There is no chance of a Kashmir settlement. But the effort has been beneficial at home and hasn't hurt here. We were probably too optimistic. No settlement between Catholics and Huguenots was possible fifteen years after the St. Bartholomew massacre and similarly here.

Yet there are problems ahead. And I earnestly plead for your attention for steps which will forestall them or make it possible that they be handled on something other than a crisis basis. Nehru's health and power are in serious decline and a major transition is in the offing. Some grave economic problems will grow out of the defense effort. There will be need for a patient and clear-headed view of the Indo-Pak problem. This is only a sample. In the absence of reform at State there could be serious trouble.

The simple truth is that the Department's handling of this part of the world is incompetent in an extremely self-satisfied way. While here I have generally known your state of mind and have been able to act accordingly. And the Department has never known quite to what extent we have been in touch. So I have been able to make decisions without waiting on the Department and I have been able by such action to forestall decisions that would have been trite or otherwise bad. This has been a daily matter and many of the decisions have been fairly consequential. This, no doubt, is a poor way to run a foreign policy. But in the particular circumstances it has worked. Had the Department been in normal control in these last months—I am not writing in service of my ego however exceptional that may be—we would have had a series of minor disasters, the result either of weak action, mechanical action or inaction. And certainly we would have lost a great deal of ground.

The whole State Department lacks confident and intelligent leadership which is conservative on policies worth conserving and which can break with the *cliches* when this is called for. There should be no mystery as to why we are doing poorly on foreign policy. The major reason is poor leadership.

But the direction for this part of the world is a special disaster. The only problems that have really baffled me in these last months have all been associated with the peculiar incapacity of this part of the Department for prompt and politically competent action. The air defense arrangements have been seven long months in the making—seven months since you gave your approval. They could have been brought off with real determination and no real effort in two. I have been able to hold the matter open here (I hope) only by most major effort. There has been a similar inability to sense the Indian urgency on military matters and this has given the Soviets their chance to move in. I do not want to see a big military program here. It would cost us money and give rise to dangerous tax weariness from the larger Indian share—something very bad in a poor country and already a threat. But firm assurances of a moderate program in early spring would have had far more effect than a bigger one now and might have forestalled the turn to the Soviets. (And in the end it was the Pentagon and White House that got the action.) "We do not believe we will be ready to discuss this matter before . . ." "You should inform the Indians that the matter is now under study." "Careful consideration is being given . . ." For Christ's sake! The Department's instructions on Kashmir were also the product of academic and dilettante meetings with the British and you can count yourself fortunate that you never saw them. I was able to control this, however. The one proposal—an academic exercise outlining the basic *Elements* of a settlement—that did get away from me was a minor calamity on both sides.

The focus of the problem is Phil Talbot.[158] He is amiable, well-intentioned and, generally speaking, has the right view of policy. But he is no good. He is frightened of his own shadow and politically innocent. You used to complain to me about the type of liberal who was for all better things, against all bad and who was devoid either of political capacity or the ability to get things done. Should this matter ever come up again it will be hard for me not to offer my own examples. Grant,[159] Phil's deputy, a rather graceless type and insecure, is actually better. He has a sense of size and can make up his mind. But he is not good enough either. The people down the line are actually very much better.

Chester[160] will not be able to operate with the same confidence that I have. And the Department will not exaggerate his pipeline to you as with some encouragement it has in my case. Accordingly, I urge that the administration of this part of the Department be got into order. In accordance with your well-known preference for affirmative suggestions, one thought is to put Bill Gaud in charge of both political and economic policy in this part of the world. He has a good mind, a blunt, profane approach to action and is without fear. Alternatively Bill Bundy might be brought over from Defense. Bill is also intelligent and willing to act. He shoots from the hip on occasion but usually in the right direction.[161]

I have discovered in these last two and a half years that the U.S.I.A.,[162] the Defense Department and even, for God's sake, the pre-Bell A.I.D.[163] function better than does the State Department. This is partly mental. The U.S.I.A. has been pummelled in the past to the point that it has a great desire for achievement. And whereas the State Department considers foreign policy something which is to be conducted largely for the convenience and enjoyment of the people in Washington, the Washington end of U.S.I.A. functions for the purpose of serving the field. I must say also that in the case of U.S.I.A., D.O.D. and now at A.I.D., one also sees the importance of strong and clear-headed leadership.

Yours faithfully,
John Kenneth Galbraith

A Word of Thanks

More than in the case of most, I am an author indebted to others. The John F. Kennedy Library in Boston began the publication process of this book by assembling and sending me this correspondence— a generous exercise of historical effort. Then it was the Harvard University Press, and there the distinguished Aïda Donald, who put forward the idea of publication and who selected James Goodman, then of the Harvard University History Department and now associate professor of history at Rutgers University, as the informed, competent, and conscientious editor. The arrangement of the letters and, as I've elsewhere noted, the spacious notes are, with my rare amendments, his. Only a very generous scholar brings his time and talent so to the support of a colleague.

As has been the case before with my work, Andrea Williams, my friend and diversely talented associate for nearly forty years, saw this book from the first bundle of typescripts to its final form. Sylvia Baldwin, my secretary and general assistant, also commands my thanks. So, and especially, does Catherine Galbraith, my wife and intellectual support for all of the last sixty years. To her, as always before, not alone my thanks but my love.

Editor's Note

In the spring of 1995, Aïda Donald, Assistant Director and Editor-in-Chief of Harvard University Press, asked me to work with John Kenneth Galbraith on the annotations for this collection of his letters to John F. Kennedy.

Galbraith is a writer with great respect for the intelligence and resources of his readers, and it is his sense that most of these letters speak for themselves. So we tread lightly, trying to keep the notes true to the spirit and style of the notes he added to his journal of the Kennedy years, which he published in 1969 as *Ambassador's Journal*. We drew liberally from *Ambassador's Journal* and from Galbraith's memoir, *A Life in Our Times;* from the brief notes with which he introduced some of the letters when he submitted them to the Press; and from the conversations about these letters that we have had over the past two years. Where we thought readers might appreciate more detail or background, we turned to, and cited, some standard and widely available sources.

A number of these letters were published in *Ambassador's Journal,* and as Galbraith noted in the introduction to that book, he deleted a few passages before publishing them there. Where the typescripts Galbraith submitted for publication contained passages deleted from *Ambassador's Journal,* we have restored the original text. But not all of them did, and readers interested in the original text of each and every letter from India would do well to compare the letters in this volume to the originals in the John F. Kennedy Library.

Notes

I. POLITICS

1. In August 1959, *Esquire*'s Harold Hayes asked 200 "outstanding men of ideas" who they preferred for president in 1960 and what they thought the "important issues" should be. Without an early discussion of issues, Hayes feared, there might be none at all, for once the campaign was underway, public discussion was likely to be fixed on the personalities of the candidates.
2. A diary I had kept on my trip to the USSR and India in the spring of 1959.
3. California governor Edmund G. (Pat) Brown; Michigan governor G. Mennen (Soapy) Williams, later assistant secretary of state for African affairs under President Kennedy; and New York mayor Robert F. Wagner, all of whom were candidates for the Democratic Party's presidential nomination.
4. Graham Barden and Phillip Landrum, conservative congressmen from North Carolina and Georgia, respectively.
5. Drew Pearson was a noted Washington journalist who had compiled an account of those working with Kennedy; Archibald Cox was a professor of law at Harvard and a Kennedy campaign aide.
6. In Alma Ata, I was attacked by a fierce dog, which tore a sizable chunk of flesh from the inside of my leg. See John Kenneth Galbraith, *A Life in Our Times* (Boston: Houghton Mifflin, 1981), pp. 366–367.
7. The headline of the *Harvard Crimson* on December 17, 1959, was "Galbraith Picks Kennedy In Recent 'Esquire' Poll." Among the faculty polled, the only other Kennedy supporter was Crane Brinton, a professor of history. Paul J. Tillich backed Adlai Stevenson, as did Louis M. Lyons, curator of the Nieman Fellowships; historian Arthur M. Schlesinger, Sr., backed Hubert Humphrey; Stanley F. Teele, dean of the Harvard Business School, backed Richard Nixon; and sociologist David Riesman warned readers against "contemporary political complacency," though he himself did not name a presidential favorite.
8. In the late 1950s there was much discussion of the problem of overpopulation in the developing world. On November 27, 1959, a few days after six-

teen U.S. Roman Catholic bishops declared the U.S. Catholic church firmly against the use of foreign aid funds to promote artificial birth control in less-developed countries, a *New York Times* reporter asked Senator Kennedy for his position. "I think it would be a mistake for the United States Government to attempt to advocate the limitation of the population of under-developed countries," he said. "This problem involves important social and economic questions which must be solved by the people of those countries themselves. For the United States to intervene on this basis would involve a kind of mean paternalism, which I think they would find most objectionable." Kennedy said he had held this view for many years, but that as president he would make his decisions based on his estimation of the best interests of the United States. A heated public debate ensued, with all the presidential hopefuls and many other political and religious leaders taking positions on the question of U.S. aid for birth control programs and even the question of U.S. distribution of birth control information abroad. At a news conference on December 2, President Eisenhower announced that he would prohibit the use of foreign aid funds to promote birth control. On December 6, Mrs. Franklin D. (Eleanor) Roosevelt insisted that each country should be free to decide the issue for itself. See the *New York Times*, November 17–December 30, 1959. A few months later, on "Meet the Press," Kennedy was asked what the United States should do to help countries in which population was outstripping production. The United States and other powers, he said, ought to help them "get ahead of their population increase. If they make a judgment that they want to limit their population under those conditions, that is a judgment they should make, and economic assistance which we give permits them to make that judgment, if that is their choice." See Arthur M. Schlesinger, Jr., *A Thousand Days: John F. Kennedy in the White House* (Boston: Houghton Mifflin, 1965), pp. 601–602.

9. Between December 1959 and June 1960, I was in Switzerland working on *The New Industrial State,* a book I did not publish until 1967.

10. Abram Chayes, professor of law at Harvard and soon to be a legal adviser at the State Department under President Kennedy; Theodore (Ted) Sorensen, Kennedy aide and speechwriter and later special counsel to President Kennedy.

11. The 1960 Democratic National Convention was held in Los Angeles in July. I was a Kennedy floor manager, in charge of the delegations west of the Mississippi and north of the Southwest. I came back to Massachusetts after the nomination but before the acceptance speech. See Galbraith, *A Life in Our Times,* pp. 378–379.

12. A memorandum now lost to history.

13. Soviet premier Nikita Khrushchev.

14. Presidential campaigns of Adlai E. Stevenson in 1952 and 1956. Stevenson was to become U.S. ambassador to the United Nations under Kennedy.

15. Willard Wirtz, law partner and campaign aide of Adlai Stevenson, under-secretary and later secretary of labor under President Kennedy. He was, in fact, a good man and a good friend.

16. Bernard Baruch, financier, chairman of the War Industries Board under Woodrow Wilson and a volunteer adviser to presidents from Franklin Roosevelt to Lyndon Johnson. Baruch died in 1965. See Galbraith, *A Life in Our Times,* pp. 130–134.

17. Among the Kennedy people, I, at the age of fifty-one plus, was an elder statesman.

18. Thomas E. Dewey, former governor of New York and unsuccessful presidential candidate in 1944 and 1948, was then campaigning for Richard Nixon.

19. Alexander Throttlebottom, hapless vice-president in the 1931 musical, *Of Thee I Sing.*

20. Hugh Gaitskell, a dominant leader in the English Labour Party after World War II, a brilliant man, a great friend of Kennedy's and of mine.

21. For a short description of this party and my role in the campaign more generally, see Galbraith, *A Life in Our Times,* pp. 372–388.

22. The first Kennedy-Nixon debate was held in Chicago on September 26, 1960. Kennedy had called to ask me to come to a pre-debate discussion. See Galbraith, *A Life in Our Times,* p. 385.

23. Henry M. (Scoop) Jackson, senator from Washington; Paul Ziffren, Los Angeles lawyer and leading Democratic Party light; Ralph W. Yarborough, senator from Texas.

24. Walter Reuther, president of the United Auto Workers from 1946 to 1970; Chester Bowles, an old friend from price control days in World War II, ambassador to India under President Truman, undersecretary of state under Kennedy in 1961, and then ambassador to India again when I stepped down in 1963. Reuther and Bowles were both articulate liberal Democrats.

25. Arthur M. Schlesinger, Jr., historian, special assistant to President Kennedy and close associate of Robert Kennedy. For years he was my Cambridge neighbor; he remains a close friend.

26. A month later, Kennedy asked me to be ambassador to India: "This morning JFK called and, in characteristic rapid-fire fashion, asked me my views on about a dozen candidates for various posts. The most interesting were Bundy for State and McNamara for Treasury. Then he told me he wanted me to go to India. I expressed my pleasure and then said I wanted to put a plain question to him: 'Would that be more useful than the Senate with the prospect of bringing some decency back to Massachusetts Democratic politics?' He said yes, 'by a factor of five to one.' Freshman senators are not very useful; did I really want to spend my time with Massachusetts politicians whom he described amiably as 'that gang of thieves.' I told him I

would not raise the matter again." John Kenneth Galbraith, *Ambassador's Journal* (Boston: Houghton Mifflin, 1969), pp. 1–2.

27. President Kennedy's inaugural address, the best remembered since that of FDR, was the work of his closest aide, Theodore Sorensen, and much more of the new president himself. But others were called to help as was I. I saw several drafts. Arthur Schlesinger, Jr., and I talked about it constantly and we did a lot of work on it. I did mostly editorial work, including maybe the final review. My memory of specific contributions has dimmed. I did add to a list of the tasks awaiting the country the words, "But let us begin." Thinking that the speech might be a trifle too belligerent in tone, I contributed the words, "Let us never negotiate out of fear. But let us never fear to negotiate." On television that day John Steinbeck, with whom I attended the proceedings, said in a voice from off camera that that was the best line in the speech, but, as shown, it sounded as if I were speaking. Kennedy called to congratulate me on an epochal exercise in self-promotion. Oddly, I was innocent.

28. Arthur Schlesinger, Jr.; Walt Rostow, chairman of the policy planning council at the State Department from 1961 to 1966, when he became a special assistant to President Johnson. My later reference to Walpurgis and the three-toed sloth was not, I judge, meant seriously.

29. Franklin D. Roosevelt's "Good Neighbor" policy, the formal abandonment of the authority to intervene in the internal affairs of Latin American states, an authority most forcefully articulated by Theodore Roosevelt's "corollary" to the Monroe Doctrine. In practice, of course, we continued to intervene.

30. The economy was slack in the winter of 1961. Arthur Goldberg, my longtime friend and the new secretary of labor, had made a tour of Detroit to show his concern for the jobless. I was then awaiting my departure to India and dispensing a not inconsiderable amount of free advice.

31. Eleanor Roosevelt; Bernard Baruch, see note 16.

32. This is probably a letter that I had drafted for Kennedy in the White House. James Conant, former president of Harvard University and ambassador to the Federal Republic of Germany, and I had sponsored the president for membership in Washington, D.C.'s Cosmos Club. But while the president's application was pending, the club rejected the application of Carl Rowan, who was black and who was also a very distinguished journalist and later deputy assistant secretary of state for public affairs under Kennedy. That put Kennedy in the position of joining a club that had no black members and that had just denied membership to a most distinguished black citizen. I called President Kennedy's press secretary, Pierre Salinger, and volunteered to resign from the club to get the president off the hook. Salinger agreed that I should resign but advised that I not do it for that reason—just resign and let the president's role be passive. So I resigned from the club. That left Kennedy without a sponsor and left the

whole question moot. Some months later, I applied for re-admission and was rejected. See also Galbraith, *Ambassador's Journal*, pp. 297–298.

33. See Part III, note 133.

34. Then the editorial page editor of the *New York Times*.

35. Richard Nixon, *Six Crises* (New York: Doubleday, 1962).

36. Kennedy "freely discussed ideas the mention of which would make most men shudder. Last summer during the visit of President Sarvepalli Radhakrishnan of India, in a social moment before a formal dinner, mention was made of some woman politician. He turned and asked me why there had been so few women politicians of importance—whether women were poorly adapted to the political art. Here surely was a politically ticklish subject; women are half the voting population and might not react well to wonder at their political shortcomings." Galbraith, *Ambassador's Journal*, p. 630.

37. Bernard Baruch, see note 16. See also my previous letters of March 16, 1961, pp. 17–18.

II. ECONOMICS

1. In his presidential campaign, Kennedy criticized the tight money policies of the Republicans. He promised a combination of lower interest rates, a short leash on spending, and a budget surplus when the economy was strong, all allowing faster growth without inflation.

2. In response to rumors that, if elected, Kennedy would devalue the dollar, London speculators began buying gold and the price soared eventually to $40 an ounce. On October 31, Kennedy announced, "If elected President, I shall not devalue the dollar from the present rate," calming the money markets. The pledge to defend the dollar was not what I (and others in the administration) would have wished. See Allen J. Matusow, *The Unraveling of America* (New York: Harper & Row, 1984), pp. 43–44.

3. This paragraph shows how an economist can get politically involved. There is a certain adjustment of economics to political necessity. "A Democratic Administration will also display greater economic fiscal responsibility . . . We will spend less on agriculture." There was no chance that we would do that. "We will put the health program under Social Security with its own source of revenue." That was a far-out thought. This is much more of a balanced budget case than I myself would make.

4. John J. McCloy was assistant secretary of war during World War II, a former president of the World Bank, a former U.S. high commissioner for Germany, and was soon to be President Kennedy's principal arms control adviser. Douglas Dillon was a New York investment banker, a Republican, ambassador to France and an assistant secretary of state under President Eisenhower, and, despite my reservations, became secretary of the treasury under Kennedy. He has long been a good friend.

5. Richard Bolling, congressman from Missouri; Albert Gore, Sr., senator from Tennessee and an old friend; Henry Reuss, congressman from Wisconsin and another old friend.
6. Paul Douglas, senator from Illinois.
7. In 1936, FDR won reelection by a landslide, winning 46 states and 523 electoral votes and carrying huge Democratic majorities into Congress on his coattails. His Republican opponent, Kansan Alfred Landon, won only Vermont and Maine.
8. Henry Wallace, secretary of agriculture, then vice president, and finally secretary of commerce under FDR; in 1948, Wallace was the Progressive Party's candidate for president.
9. Orville Freeman, then in his last days as governor of Minnesota, soon to be President Kennedy's secretary of agriculture. See my letter of December 30, 1960, and note 15.
10. George McGovern, then congressman from South Dakota, soon to be head of Kennedy's Food for Peace program, later senator and, in 1972, the Democratic Party's presidential candidate.
11. In an interview with *U.S. News & World Report* published on November 21, 1960, I had proposed a "tripartite guiding group—labor, management, and public"—to set standards for wages and prices that would be consistent with price stability.
12. Walter Reuther, president of the United Auto Workers; David Dubinsky, president of the International Ladies' Garment Workers' Union; David J. McDonald, head of the United Steelworkers' Union; George Meany, president of the American Federation of Labor–Congress of Industrial Organizations. The group and the task force were evidently never formed.
13. Meyer (Mike) Feldman was a member of the Kennedy senatorial and campaign staffs and deputy special counsel to President Kennedy and later President Johnson. Stanley S. Surrey, a professor of law at Harvard, who became assistant secretary for tax policy in the Department of the Treasury under President Kennedy.
14. I had enclosed my article, "Some Thoughts on Public Policy and [the] Dollar Problem," *Commercial and Financial Chronicle,* December 1, 1960.
15. I was one of the advocates, I expect the principal advocate, of Orville Freeman, who had just finished his term as governor of Minnesota, for secretary of agriculture. Kennedy called me up to say he was appointing Freeman. Freeman flew down to Washington to talk with him and then Kennedy called me up again and said to go out to see Freeman, get any views he had, and persuade him not to state them until he got to Washington. I had a full discussion with Freeman. The secretary of agriculture was a decisive figure at that time, much more important than now, and I went over the whole range of agricultural matters, which in those days was something with which I was in close touch. I was the agricultural economist, among other things, at Harvard. Freeman had been a governor, and

a good governor, but like many midwestern governors, he was not closely involved with agricultural legislation. (I had found in working with Adlai Stevenson [a former governor of Illinois], for example, how little Stevenson knew about farm policy.) This letter reports on what I told Freeman to say as to policy, but Freeman was not to say it. There is a strong possibility that Kennedy did not read it. The text in the original letter, in item 10, reads, "food supplies." Meant was "food surplus."

16. Ezra Taft Benson, secretary of agriculture under Eisenhower, an extreme conservative, whose opposition to firm agricultural price supports and many other forms of government intervention in agriculture angered many farmers and their congressmen, including Republican congressmen.

17. Robert V. Roosa, notably influential undersecretary of the treasury for monetary affairs under Kennedy.

18. William McChesney Martin, Jr., chairman of the Federal Reserve Board.

19. This letter has not survived.

20. Evidently I wrote this memorandum during a trip back to Washington, where, regularly, I was asked by the president for recommendations on economic policy and, quite possibly, offered a few without being asked. My feeling that high interest rates are often advanced for high purpose but in reality are to reward money-lenders and the affluent is here evident.

21. In early 1962, with the contract between U.S. Steel and its unions set to expire and the Kennedy administration worried about the effect of wage and price increases on inflation, Secretary of Labor Arthur Goldberg pressed the steel unions to accept a smaller hourly wage increase than they had hoped for. The administration expected that the company would respond to labor's anti-inflation concessions responsibly by leaving the price of steel where it was. But in April, immediately after the contract was signed, U.S. Steel announced a price increase of $6 a ton, and a number of other large companies followed suit. President Kennedy characterized the increase as "a wholly unjustifiable and irresponsible defiance of the public interest" by "a tiny handful of steel executives whose pursuit of private power and profit exceeds their sense of public responsibility." He asked a grand jury to investigate price fixing and the Federal Trade Commission to determine if the company had violated antitrust laws. The Defense Department announced it would purchase steel only from companies that had not raised prices. U.S. Steel rolled back its prices. See Matusow, *The Unraveling of America,* pp. 39–41; Arthur M. Schlesinger, Jr., *A Thousand Days: John F. Kennedy in the White House* (Boston: Houghton Mifflin, 1965), pp. 634–640; and John Morton Blum, *Years of Discord: American Politics and Society, 1961–1974* (New York: W. W. Norton, 1991), pp. 58–60.

22. On May 28, 1962, the Dow Jones industrial average lost 35 points, the largest one-day drop since "Black Monday," October 28, 1929. The mar-

ket had been declining in fits and starts for a month, and it would continue
to decline until the end of June, by which time it had lost 27 percent of its
value in six months.

23. John Kenneth Galbraith, *The Great Crash, 1929* (Boston: Houghton
Mifflin, 1955; second edition, 1961).

24. Cf. Galbraith, *Ambassador's Journal,* pp. 393–394.

25. The "New Economists" in the administration, led by Walter Heller, chairman of the Council of Economic Advisers, had been pressing Kennedy for
a tax cut for nearly two years. Good Keynesians, they believed that the
government should spur a sluggish economy with tax cuts and spending increases and tame an overheated economy with tax increases and spending
cuts. I was against the tax cut, arguing instead for increases in social spending. Government spending would pump money into the economy and
spread the benefits around. Tax cuts disproportionately benefit the
wealthy. Kennedy eventually went for a tax cut, the largest in U.S. history.
See note 26.

26. In August 1962, President Kennedy went on national television to give a
lecture on economics. He promised that in January 1963, in order to
stimulate the economy and remove a significant barrier to full employment, he would ask Congress to enact a major ($10 billion) tax reduction.
I expressed some of my reservations in this letter. Although Kennedy did
not live to see the day, a tax cut was enacted by Congress in early 1964.
For a good introduction to economic policy and policy debates during the
Kennedy administration, see Matusow, *The Unraveling of America,*
pp. 30–59.

27. Russell A. Nixon, instructor in economics at Harvard, "a handsome, intelligent man who numbered among his students in beginning economics and
later in labor economics the young John F. Kennedy. Whenever, as President, Kennedy encountered an arcane economic term or concept, it was
his pleasure, were he in some trustworthy Harvard presence, to put his
hand to the side of his mouth and say, 'Why do you suppose Russ Nixon
didn't teach me that?'" John Kenneth Galbraith, *A Life in Our Times* (Boston: Houghton Mifflin, 1981), p. 96.

28. Billy Graham, of course, did not use the phrase "Christ-bitten"; that was
an invention of mine.

29. Bernard Baruch, see Part I, note 16.

30. Chester Bowles, see Part I, note 24.

31. In early October 1963, Kennedy announced that the United States government would not prevent a private sale of 150 million bushels of wheat to
the Soviet Union and its allies.

32. President Kennedy had long hoped for a comprehensive nuclear test ban.
But critics in the military and in Congress feared not just that a ban would
cripple our nuclear program but also that, without regular on-site inspections, the Soviet Union would cheat. Only through on-site inspections,

they claimed, could we distinguish between earthquakes and underground tests and be sure the Soviets complied with a comprehensive ban. (Tests in the atmosphere and the ocean we could monitor from outside the Soviet Union.) The Soviets, for their part, feared that regular on-site inspections would give U.S. spies free rein. In the end, the administration settled for a limited nuclear test ban, which prohibited tests in the atmosphere, outer space, and under the seas. The Senate ratified the ban by a vote of 80–19 on September 24, 1963.

III. FOREIGN AFFAIRS

1. Another travel diary I shared with Senator Kennedy; Kennedy meant Phileas Fogg, the eccentric traveler in Jules Verne's novel, *Around the World in Eighty Days* (1872); John Foster Dulles, of course, was secretary of state under President Eisenhower.
2. See Part I, note 26.
3. Massachusetts General Hospital.
4. This I thought at the time one of the more urgent letters I had ever written. I had just that day learned of the impending invasion of Cuba, what was to become known as the Bay-of-Pigs disaster. My source, Chester Bowles, then undersecretary of state, had told me in the utmost confidence. I thought that if I were specific as to my fears, I would invite questions as to where I got my information, and as to who had breached the imposing wall of secrecy. So I put my concern as here, omitting specific reference to Castro and Cuba. The letter, needless to say, had no effect; perhaps, as I now reflect, it was more to salve my own conscience than to change or reverse the by-then strongly determined flow of events. I left for India the following day.
5. In November 1950, five months into the Korean War, U.S. forces under the direction of General Douglas MacArthur crossed the 38th parallel into North Korea and drove the North Korean army back to the Yalu River, which separates North Korea and China. The invasion of North Korea transformed a war to regain control of South Korea into a war to unite the entire Korean peninsula, or so it seemed. The action, which brought China into the war, ultimately failed.
6. John Foster Dulles was secretary of state in 1954, when the United States was deeply involved in Colonel Carlos Castillo Armas's overthrow of the Guatemalan government of Jacobo Arbenz Guzman, who was believed to be a Communist.
7. In May 1960, on the eve of a summit meeting between the United States and the USSR, the Soviets shot down a U.S. U-2 spy plane. The summit was a failure, and many of us questioned the wisdom of sending up the plane at so delicate a moment in U.S.–USSR diplomacy.
8. Jawaharlal Nehru, prime minister of India, 1947–1964. Many Americans

and many in the Kennedy administration considered Nehru dangerously unconcerned about the Communists.

9. Cf. John Kenneth Galbraith, *Ambassador's Journal* (Boston: Houghton Mifflin, 1969), pp. 73–77.

10. "This wording implies that the idea of the letters came from me. However, my memory is quite clear that the president proposed them—following, though I am less certain of this, some expression of doubt as to how an ambassador really employed himself." Galbraith, *Ambassador's Journal*, pp. xiv–xv, 74; the quote comes from p. 74.

11. Charles-Maurice de Talleyrand, French diplomat and politician.

12. "I had taken up with him, as had others, the matter of rescuing the Nubian monuments, including Abu Simbel, from the Nile waters rising behind the new Aswan Dam." Galbraith, *Ambassador's Journal*, p. 75. PL 480 was a rupee fund from the sale of food to the Indians that was not convertible into dollars and was, therefore, available only for expenditures in India.

13. Chester Bowles, see Part I, note 24; John Sherman Cooper, senator from Kentucky, ambassador to India under Eisenhower and a personal friend; Ellsworth Bunker, another friend and former ambassador to India and, later, ambassador to South Vietnam.

14. After the Congo achieved its independence from France in 1960, civil war broke out. United Nations forces sought to restore order. There was concern in the Kennedy administration that the conflict there might lead to a confrontation between the United States and the USSR. See Arthur M. Schlesinger, Jr., *A Thousand Days: John F. Kennedy in the White House* (Boston: Houghton Mifflin, 1965), pp. 574–579.

15. Rajeshwar Dayal, Indian high commissioner to Pakistan, later ambassador to France; "Clare H. Timberlake, a professional Foreign Service officer, had previously served in India, where he had aroused the suspicion of Nehru in connection with sundry Cold War maneuvers. Accordingly, in the Congo, he was much suspected by the Indians." Galbraith, *Ambassador's Journal*, p. 50.

16. William McChesney Martin, Jr., chairman of the Federal Reserve Board, who believed, as do all Federal Reserve Board chairmen, in the Fed's complete independence.

17. Cf. Galbraith, *Ambassador's Journal*, pp. 89–91.

18. The Cubans routed the CIA-sponsored invasion of Cuba by Cuban exiles at the Bay of Pigs on April 17, 1961. I wrote this letter in the aftermath of the fiasco. I tactfully omitted reference to my unduly general letter of warning of April 3—and also to the demonstrators who, for a time, descended on the American Embassy in India.

19. This policy paper was never written.

20. "A tactful reference, for Peru does not accredit an ambassador to India." Galbraith, *Ambassador's Journal*, p. 90.

21. This reference to underdeveloped countries and overdeveloped women is far from graceful and also far from original. I first heard it from Adlai Stevenson, who was describing the people he had encountered during a stay on the Riviera.

22. Foster Furcolo, recently retired governor of Massachusetts.

23. J. William Fulbright, senator from Arkansas and a personal friend, who had long insisted that American ambassadors be competent in the language of the country to which they were going.

24. Sargent Shriver, brother-in-law of the President, the first director of the Peace Corps and then, concurrently, director of the Office of Economic Opportunity.

25. Cf. Galbraith, *Ambassador's Journal*, pp. 107–111.

26. When Kennedy took office, the anti-Communist government of Laos, like the anti-Communist government of South Vietnam, was in jeopardy. In response to guerrilla action by Pathet Lao Communist forces, the United States had increased its military presence; by April 1961, we had over 300 military advisers there. I was deeply concerned in those days with seeking solutions in Laos and elsewhere in Indochina that would limit or avoid our involvement. New Delhi was a critical center, for the Indians chaired the International Control Commission, which had been established under the earlier Geneva Accords for bringing peace to the area. As noted, I did not think my efforts decisive.

27. John Foster Dulles; see note 1.

28. The "adventuresome and spooky enterprises" were, needless to say, those of the CIA, in this case support to guerrillas of indifferent personal hygiene who were raiding from Nepal into Tibet and being supplied by flights over India from Bangkok. With the president's support these flights were brought to an end as, to the grave distress of the more sensitive defenders of the free world in Washington, were various covert activities in India. See also Galbraith, *A Life in Our Times*, pp. 389–398.

29. Arthur M. Schlesinger, Jr.; see Part I, note 25.

30. A Chicago business complex, owned by the Kennedy family.

31. Edward R. Murrow, celebrated journalist, broadcaster, and news analyst with CBS and head of the United States Information Agency under Kennedy. "The President, as I later learned, read this to Ed Murrow over the telephone in what Ed described as the most difficult single telephone call of his life. It pleased the president to imply that Murrow had written it personally. Presently the file diminished radically in size. Previously anything that might offend a right-wing congressman was deleted. Now anything that might offend me had also to go. Not much was left between." Galbraith, *Ambassador's Journal*, p. 110.

32. Lawrence O'Brien, special assistant to President Kennedy for congressional relations.

33. Sargent Shriver, see note 24.
34. V. K. Krishna Menon. "Following Independence, he became Indian high commissioner in London and then returned to a political career in India where he finally became minister of defense. During these years he became widely known in the United States as the perennial leader of the Indian delegation to the General Assembly of the United Nations and as a participant in numerous other international conferences, at all of which he was an eloquent, frequent and unsparing critic of American policy." Galbraith, *Ambassador's Journal*, p. 84.
35. Vice-President Lyndon Baines Johnson.
36. cf. Galbraith, *Ambassador's Journal,* pp. 151–154.
37. "This usage, I should perhaps explain to Indian readers, bears no relation to nineteenth century imperial language. It is an American slang form. 'You were in Boston. How did you find the natives?'" Galbraith, *Ambassador's Journal,* p. 151.
38. Kennedy met with Khrushchev in Vienna in June 1961. He had hoped to negotiate a cease-fire in Laos and to reach agreement on the terms for a comprehensive test ban treaty at the test ban talks ongoing in Geneva. But though they came to a preliminary agreement on the neutralization of Laos, Khrushchev rejected the idea of a comprehensive test ban. The USSR, Khrushchev said, wanted total disarmament; in the meantime, U.S. proposals for on-site inspections were unacceptable. Worse, and more foreboding, was Khrushchev's talk of the ultimate triumph of Communism and his menacing lecture about Berlin. Sixteen years after the end of World War II, Khrushchev complained, the West had failed to sign a peace treaty with Germany. Yet West Germany had become a dominant NATO power, and there were British, French, and U.S. troops in West Berlin, which put them in the heart of East Germany. Khrushchev wanted a German peace treaty, making Berlin a free city. If the West refused to negotiate a peace treaty, the Soviet Union would go it alone. See Schlesinger, *A Thousand Days,* pp. 358–374; Theodore Sorensen, *Kennedy* (New York, Harper & Row, 1965), pp. 583–601; and Richard Reeves, *President Kennedy: Profile of Power* (New York: Simon and Schuster, 1993), pp. 156–184.
39. The new China policy refers to "[a] proposal by the President that we open up a new channel of communication with Peking. For various reasons, the matter was not pursued. The 'dust-up' refers to rumors that the Administration was moving to revise the China policy." Galbraith, *Ambassador's Journal,* p. 152. Earlier in the year, my nomination as ambassador to India was held up a bit because I had advocated the recognition of Red China and that caused a considerable fuss on Capitol Hill. Actually I had qualified my statement about recognizing the Chinese. I had said that we should do so only when they recognize the separate existence of Formosa, as it then was, Taiwan. But any suggestion in those days that you were in

favor of recognizing Red China was taken by the right-wing Republicans as an indication of crypto-Bolshevism.

40. See note 26.

41. Harry Hopkins, chief aide to FDR.

42. Dean Acheson, secretary of state in the Truman administration and an informal adviser to President Kennedy.

43. Since 1947, Kashmir had been a persistent source of trouble between India and Pakistan, including undeclared wars in 1947, 1948, and 1951. Kashmir's Maharaja was Hindu, but 75 percent of its population was Muslim. A United Nations–sponsored cease-fire in 1949 led to the partitioning of the state into a Pakistani section, Azad Kashmir, and the Indian state of Jammu and Kashmir. At a news conference on June 30, 1961, Nehru called on Pakistan to withdraw from that part of Kashmir occupied by the Pakistani army, a withdrawal which Nehru claimed the Security Council had called for eight years earlier. Nehru and Lt. General K. M. Sheikh, Pakistani minister for rehabilitation, states and frontier regions, held talks on July 8, 1961, but the talks ended inconclusively, with General Sheikh calling for the withdrawal of the Indian army from the region and claiming that earlier hopes that the problem could be resolved had been "obliterated." The Kashmir question was repeatedly before the United Nations; in 1965, it led to a declared war between India and Pakistan.

44. Ngo Dinh Diem, prime minister of South Vietnam from 1954 to 1963, when he was assassinated during a coup d'etat staged by dissident generals. The United States, which had earlier been a strong supporter of Diem, was complicit in the coup.

45. Cf. Galbraith, *Ambassador's Journal*, pp. 172–174.

46. "I had opposed our efforts to shove the British into the Common Market. The reasons for our supporting the formation of a tariff club organized to discriminate against the United States escaped me." Galbraith, *Ambassador's Journal*, p. 155.

47. Peter Thorneycroft, British Tory M.P. and minister of defense.

48. Charles De Gaulle, leader of Free French forces during World War II and president of the Republic of France from 1959 to 1969.

49. The "new air lift" was an Air Force Convair; the Dakota was the widely used name for the Douglas DC-3, which was not a high-altitude plane.

50. Cf. Galbraith, *Ambassador's Journal*, pp. 186–189.

51. Bernard Baruch, see Part I, note 16.

52. Chester Bowles, see Part I, note 24; Phillips Talbot, assistant secretary of state for Near East and South Asian affairs and my immediate point of contact in the State Department. See Galbraith, *A Life in Our Times*, pp. 401–403, 415–416.

53. "The World War II Office of Price Administration of which he became the head in 1943 shortly after my own much applauded withdrawal [as dep-

uty in charge of price control] . . ." Galbraith, *Ambassador's Journal,* p. 187.

54. See note 34.
55. Wayne Morse, a strongly opinionated senator from Oregon and my good friend.
56. Arthur M. Schlesinger, Jr.; W. Averell Harriman, former governor of New York, ambassador-at-large under President Kennedy and then President Johnson, and a longtime personal friend.
57. Cf. Galbraith, *Ambassador's Journal,* pp. 195–196.
58. "An offensive official usage for which I weep." Galbraith, *Ambassador's Journal,* p. 195.
59. Edward Maffitt, deputy chief of mission in New Delhi and M. J. Desai, India's foreign secretary.
60. Antonio de Oliveira Salazar, Portuguese dictator; Chiang Kai-shek of Nationalist China (Taiwan, formerly Formosa); Sarit Thanarat, prime minister of Thailand.
61. General Mohammad Ayub Khan, president of Pakistan.
62. Cf. Galbraith, *Ambassador's Journal,* pp. 210–212.
63. A few weeks earlier, in August 1961, in order to stop the mass defections of East Berliners to the West, and to prevent East Berliners from commuting to jobs in West Berlin, the Soviets had taken over crossing points in East Berlin and built and fortified the famous twenty-nine-mile concrete wall, the Berlin Wall, between the eastern and western sections of the city.
64. Walter Ulbricht, East German leader.
65. Chiang Kai-shek, leader of Nationalist China (Taiwan).
66. Cf. Galbraith, *Ambassador's Journal,* pp. 223–225.
67. John Foster Dulles. See note 1.
68. Nehru was to visit the United States in November 1961.
69. Leon Henderson, under whom I served in the Office of Price Administration during World War II.
70. I had been sent by Kennedy to Vietnam. Cincpac refers to a meeting with the commander-in-chief of the Pacific, Harry Felt.
71. Communist insurgents in South Vietnam.
72. GVN, Government of (South) Vietnam.
73. Ngo Dinh Diem. See note 44.
74. SVN, South Vietnam.
75. RVN, Republic of Vietnam (South Vietnam).
76. Frederick E. Nolting, career officer and ambassador to South Vietnam from 1961 to 1963; Lieutenant General Lionel C. McGarr, head of the Military Assistance Advisory Group.
77. Syngman Rhee, then president of South Korea.
78. In 1954, Secretary of State John Foster Dulles and the Eisenhower administration considered sending troops to South Vietnam on the eve of the French defeat at Dien Bien Phu, but ultimately decided not to intervene.

79. Dean Acheson, secretary of state in 1949, when Mao Tse-tung's Communists swept through China. President Truman sent military aid to support Chiang Kai-shek but not troops. Chiang was driven to Taiwan, and Mao came to power.

80. "The International Control Commission, consisting of Canada, Poland, and India, with the latter as chairman, was established under the authority of the 1954 Geneva Accords to limit foreign military intervention in the Indo-Chinese successor states, and otherwise enforce the terms of the Accords. It had been expelled from Laos by a right-wing government (brought in with the skilled efforts of the then American Ambassador, Mr. Graham Parsons, and the CIA) and was now sitting in India." Galbraith, *Ambassador's Journal*, p. 93.

81. Eugene Staley, president of Stanford Research Institute, whom Kennedy soon sent to Vietnam, along with several others, to evaluate Diem's economic programs.

82. John (Jack) Bell, ambassador to Guatemala.

83. Diem was overthrown in November 1963. For one view of the Kennedy administration's complicated role in the coup, see Robert S. McNamara, *In Retrospect: The Tragedy and Lessons of Vietnam* (New York: Times Books, 1995).

84. Cf. Galbraith, *Ambassador's Journal*, pp. 266–269.

85. Maxwell Taylor, sent to Vietnam as a military representative of the president to assess conditions firsthand and try to determine whether it was necessary or desirable for the United States to send troops. In 1962, Kennedy named Taylor chairman of the Joint Chiefs of Staff; in 1964, President Johnson named him U.S. ambassador to South Vietnam.

86. Ngo Dinh Diem.

87. Robert F. Wagner, mayor of New York.

88. On a West Coast trip in early November 1961, President Kennedy had criticized the political extremism of the left and the right, but especially of the right: "There have always been those on the fringes of our society who have sought to escape their own responsibility by finding a simple solution, an appealing slogan or a convenient scapegoat . . . They find treason in our churches, in our highest court, in our treatment of water. They equate the Democratic Party with the welfare state, the welfare state with socialism, socialism with Communism." Schlesinger, *A Thousand Days*, pp. 752–753.

89. Nehru had visited the United States in early November 1961, meeting with JFK at Newport and then in Washington. See Galbraith, *Ambassador's Journal*, pp. 245–253, and Schlesinger, *A Thousand Days*, pp. 522–526.

90. Arthur Schlesinger, Jr.

91. Cf. Galbraith, *Ambassador's Journal*, pp. 310–312.

92. Jacqueline Kennedy was now scheduled to arrive in New Delhi on March 12. See Galbraith, *Ambassador's Journal*, pp. 305–340.

93. "Goa, which occupied some sixty-five miles of the west, or Malabar, coast of India to the south of Bombay, constituted, along with the two small enclaves of Damao and Diu, the Portuguese Africa in India. There was no obvious reason, its greater antiquity (from 1510) apart, why it should not have become part of the Indian union, along with British and French India and the partially independent Princely States at the time of Independence. The failure of the Portuguese to yield was a major annoyance to the Indians, as was the use of Goa as a center for smuggling on a considerable scale including the whiskey that was banned by the formidable dry laws of the adjacent state of Maharashtra. Though extensively converted to Christianity, the Goanese are not ethnically distinct from the other people of India." Galbraith, *Ambassador's Journal,* pp. 274–275. In December 1961, the Indian army had invaded and occupied the region; during the conflict, I urged the administration to balance its condemnation of India for its resort to force with condemnation of Portugal for its refusal to end its colonialism in India. Galbraith, *Ambassador's Journal,* pp. 276–277, 280–293. See also Schlesinger, *A Thousand Days,* pp. 526–531.

94. Harold Ross, legendary *New Yorker* editor and James Thurber, equally legendary *New Yorker* artist and writer.

95. Admiral Harry Felt, see note 70.

96. General Paul D. Harkins.

97. Winthrop Brown, ambassador to Laos.

98. Joseph Alsop, highly influential and much-feared Washington journalist, then a syndicated columnist for the *New York Herald Tribune.*

99. Cf. Galbraith, *Ambassador's Journal,* pp. 341–342. I was in Washington on a brief visit.

100. Robert McNamara, secretary of defense under Kennedy.

101. W. Averell Harriman, see note 56.

102. See note 43.

103. Agency for International Development.

104. A Kennedy retreat in Virginia.

105. Cf. Galbraith, *Ambassador's Journal,* pp. 342–344.

106. International Control Commission; see notes 26 and 80.

107. Cf. Galbraith, *Ambassador's Journal,* pp. 372–375.

108. I developed stomach trouble in December 1961, and the effects lasted for many months.

109. Dean Rusk, assistant secretary of state for Far Eastern affairs in the Truman administration, secretary of state under Kennedy and then Lyndon Johnson.

110. There had been an informal nuclear test ban in effect since November 1958, when the United States, Great Britain, and the Soviet Union opened a test ban conference in Geneva, Switzerland. In June 1961, in Vienna, Khrushchev had rejected President Kennedy's call for a comprehen-

sive test ban treaty and two months later the Soviet Union officially resumed atmospheric testing. In September 1961, the United States resumed underground testing, and in April 1962, the United States resumed testing in the Pacific Ocean. See also Part II, note 32 and Part III, note 38.

111. See note 61.

112. Phoumi Nosavan, Laotian army officer whose anti-Communist credentials earned him U.S. support.

113. The Nagas were a tribal group in India that sought its own separate Naga state.

114. "A final untactful sentence was deleted from this letter." Galbraith, *Ambassador's Journal,* p. 375.

115. David Lawrence, editor of *U.S. News & World Report* and a syndicated columnist.

116. Cf. Galbraith, *Ambassador's Journal,* pp. 395–397.

117. Carl Kaysen, on the White House staff, previously and later professor of economics at Harvard, then director of the Institute of Advanced Study at Princeton, and finally for many years a professor of economics at MIT. Ruth Montgomery, a columnist for the *New York Journal American.* Kaysen sent me a number of items. In one, a column published in the *Journal American* on March 22, 1962, Montgomery had panned my performance as host to Jackie Kennedy on her recent trip to India. Another enclosure "criticized the Administration for too much aid and attention to India for too small a reward. I was asked to comment, the implication being that the President partly agreed. The President some time before was said to have banished the *New York Herald Tribune* from the White House." Galbraith, *Ambassador's Journal,* p. 395.

118. For V. K. Krishna Menon, minister of defense, see note 34. For Goa, see note 93. In July 1961, the United States had angered India by delivering twelve F-104 jets to Pakistan (see my letter of August 15, 1961). For Kashmir, see notes 43 and 120.

119. M. J. Desai, India's foreign secretary.

120. On April 27, 1962, the United Nations Security Council had once again taken up the question of Kashmir; this was its 100th meeting on the subject, which had been on the Security Council agenda since 1948. As previously noted, Menon was a regular participant in the U.N. debate. See also note 43.

121. The long-standing tensions between China and India over their disputed Himalayan border had escalated to shooting, though as yet not much of it, that began in the middle of July 1962.

122. In 1961, the Soviet Union had offered to sell MIG fighter planes to India, a deal the United States opposed and made significant efforts to stop. "I now look back on this effort to stop the MIG deal, its congressional public relations aspect apart, as unwarranted. The planes were a great waste

of money, as were the F-104's for Pakistan, but that was the Indians' business. The foothold they provided to the Soviets in supplying military goods was not important." Galbraith, *Ambassador's Journal*, p. 383.

123. India's invasion of the ancient Portuguese colony of Goa. See note 93.

124. A proposal to underwrite the sale of British fighter planes (Lightnings) to India intended to dissuade the Indians from buying Soviet MIGs. See note 122.

125. See note 98.

126. Major General Edwin A. Walker, division commander in West Germany, who had been relieved of his command in the spring of 1961 after it was learned that he had distributed right-wing political propaganda to his troops.

127. J. B. Bury, Regius Professor of History, Cambridge University, who died in 1927.

128. At a news conference on August 1, President Kennedy said: "The Indian Government itself will make its final judgment as a sovereign power. Mr. Galbraith only attempted to suggest some of the factors which were of interest to us as a friend of India." John F. Kennedy, *Public Papers of the Presidents of the United States* (Washington, D.C.: Government Printing Office, 1962–1964), vol. 2, 1962, pp. 594–595. See also notes 122 and 124.

129. Cf. Galbraith, *Ambassador's Journal*, pp. 424–426. This confidential document was sanitized before release to the public.

130. The border conflict with China was about to turn into a war; Krishna Menon, Indian defense minister.

131. Agency for International Development.

132. "An unkind adjective justified only by the bad state of my digestive tract that day and for which I apologize to all citizens of that city. I do not believe that God has forsaken it." Galbraith, *Ambassador's Journal*, p. 426.

133. Between the Vienna summit in June 1961 and the Berlin crisis in August 1961, President Kennedy had gone on national television to announce that in order to prevent the Soviets from driving us out of Berlin, he would ask Congress for a $3.25 billion increase in military spending, call up over a hundred thousand reservists, and dramatically enlarge our civil defense program. The president's proposal for civil defense called for the construction of nuclear shelters, and many Americans were alarmed. (Many other Americans were deluded into thinking that in a fallout shelter they could survive a nuclear war.) I expressed my reservations about "Fallout Protection," a Department of Defense pamphlet, in a letter to Kennedy on November 9, 1961 (see Part I, p. 19). See also John Morton Blum, *Years of Discord: American Politics and Society, 1961–1974* (New York: W. W. Norton, 1991), p. 46; Schlesinger, *A Thousand Days,*

pp. 390–384; and Reeves, *President Kennedy,* pp. 135, 176, 180, 196, 204, 233–234, 271–272.

Here I was asking about reports of Soviet arms shipments to Cuba. Shipment of Soviet weapons to Cuba had begun in July 1962, and U-2 flights in September and early October had revealed a large build-up, which at first seemed to be, as Khrushchev repeatedly insisted, only defensive weapons. When I wrote on October 16, I, like most Americans, was unaware that two days earlier reconnaissance planes had returned with evidence—photographs of missile sites—that Khrushchev was lying. The Soviets had delivered medium-range ballistic missiles and nuclear warheads to Cuba, setting the stage for the Cuban missile crisis. On October 22, the President alerted the nation, announcing a naval blockade intended to interrupt all offensive weapons being shipped to Cuba, and warning the Soviets that the United States would respond to an attack by Cuba as if it were an attack by the USSR. To the end, Khrushchev insisted that the missiles were defensive in nature, but on October 28, he agreed to remove them. See Schlesinger, *A Thousand Days,* pp. 794–841; Blum, *Years of Discord,* pp. 76–91; and, for a more recent view based on research in Soviet as well as U.S. archives, Aleksandr V. Fursenko and Timothy Naftali, *One Hell of a Gamble: Khrushchev, Castro, and Kennedy 1958–1964* (New York: W. W. Norton, 1997).

134. On September 30, 1962, after five days of resistance by Mississippi governor Ross Barnett, James Meredith, an African American, escorted by 500 federal marshals, had entered the University of Mississippi. Students and thousands of outside agitators rioted, attacking the marshals, killing a French newsman and a bystander, wounding scores. It took a large military force to restore order.

135. The Cuban missile crisis.

136. At the end of October, "fighting broke out between the Chinese and the Indians in two areas—in the high, arid mountainous plateau region of Ladakh at the extreme northern point of the Indian diamond, and far to the east near Burma in the mountains north of Assam and the Brahmaputra River and just east of Bhutan. This territory, not organized as a state, is called the North-East Frontier Agency or NEFA. In Ladakh, the Indian defenders fought stubbornly but their performance was blanketed by the disastrous collapse in NEFA.

"My concern . . . was about equally divided between helping the Indians against the Chinese and keeping peace between the Indians and the Pakistanis. The latter had grievances against the Indians which they considered, not without reason, to have substance. The nightmare of a combined attack by Pakistan and China, with the possibility of defeat, collapse and even anarchy in India, was much on my mind. The later outbreak of hostilities between India and Pakistan showed these fears to be real." Galbraith, *Ambassador's Journal,* p. 428. For more on the war and peace, see *Ambassador's Journal,* pp. 428–523, and Galbraith, *A Life in Our Times,* pp. 420–442.

137. "This has been a long but interesting day. Washington continues totally occupied with Cuba. For a week, I have had a considerable war on my hands without a single telegram, letter, telephone call or other communication of guidance. The single exception was a message that came in today, warning me that I could not endorse the McMahon Line. The subject, it was said, was under study in Washington. I have been sending off telegrams on various urgent matters without the slightest knowledge of whether they are being received or acted upon. It is like marching troops out of the trenches and over no-man's land without knowing whether they get through or get shot down en route." Galbraith, *Ambassador's Journal,* pp. 435–436.

138. Embtel and Deptel are telegraphic communications from embassies and departments. The McMahon Line was the border between China and India established in a 1914 agreement between Arthur Henry McMahon, British foreign secretary for India, and Tibetan officials—an agreement that China did not recognize as legitimate. It stretched from Bhutan to Burma, following the crest of the high Himalayas. See Galbraith, *A Life in Our Times,* pp. 424–426.

139. Cf. Galbraith, *Ambassador's Journal,* pp. 473–476.

140. "There followed a long discussion of Indian political personalities which, along with some later references, I have deleted for reasons of taste. Another change has been made in this letter. In the private language of the State Department, the Pakistanis are sometimes referred to as 'the Paks.' It is not, I think, an agreeable usage." Galbraith, *Ambassador's Journal,* p. 473.

141. They did not. On November 21, 1962, the Chinese promised to stop shooting and to withdraw.

142. The United States, along with Great Britain, had provided arms for India during the war.

143. See note 61.

144. Walter McConaughy, assistant secretary of state for Far Eastern affairs and later ambassador to Pakistan.

145. See note 43.

146. "News also came during the course of the evening that another expendable politician was gone. Nixon was defeated in California. Meanwhile, Chub Peabody has been elected Governor of Massachusetts. I have contributed to Chub's campaigns over the years, spoken for him, and generally considered him to have one of the less promising careers in politics. He never had any program. I once urged him to admit the fact and run on the simple platform, 'Vote for Peabody, he don't steal.' He doesn't

have to conform to very high standards to be a relatively successful governor in Massachusetts. George McGovern was elected to the Senate in South Dakota, as were most of my friends elsewhere." Galbraith, *Ambassador's Journal,* p. 464.

147. Cf. Galbraith, *Ambassador's Journal,* pp. 510–514.

148. On October 31, 1962, Krishna Menon was relieved of his position as minister of defense (the prime minister took over the Defence Ministry himself). Menon was named the new minister of defense production. He fought to keep his old job, but on November 8, it was announced that he had been relieved of all jobs in the Indian government.

149. See note 136.

150. See Part II, notes 25 and 26.

151. In his 1963 State of the Union address, the president had proposed permanent reduction in the tax rates for individuals and corporations that would add up to 11 billion dollars of new tax cuts, to be phased in over three years.

152. "After Two Years—A Conversation with the President," an interview with NBC-TV correspondent Sander Vanocur, recorded on December 16, 1962, and broadcast on December 17 by all three networks.

153. Professor John D. Black, professor of agricultural economics at Harvard, who died in 1960. See Galbraith, *A Life in Our Times,* pp. 54–56.

154. Local Alsops (Joseph and Stewart) and Bartletts (Charles), by which I meant local newsmen.

155. Dr. Sarvepalli Radhakrishnan, former Oxford professor and ambassador, author, and now president of India.

156. Benson E. L. (Lane) Timmons. "He had been Deputy Chief of Mission in Stockholm. Following his tour of duty in India, the State Department proposed him for a minor NATO post in Paris. At President Kennedy's personal insistence, reflecting appreciation of his energy and instinct for accomplishment if not his tact, he was made Ambassador to Haiti." Galbraith, *Ambassador's Journal,* p. 204.

157. Pandit Madan Mohan Malaviya. "An orthodox Hindu, he was ceremoniously reborn when some eighty years old but, unhappily, died soon thereafter." Galbraith, *Ambassador's Journal,* p. 413.

158. Phillips Talbot; see note 52 and also Galbraith, *A Life in Our Times,* pp. 424–426.

159. James Grant, deputy assistant secretary of state.

160. Chester Bowles, see Part I, note 24.

161. William Gaud, regional (Middle East) director of the Agency for International Development, of which he later became head; William Bundy, deputy assistant secretary of defense for international security affairs; in October JFK named him assistant secretary of defense for the same. William Bundy was also the brother of McGeorge Bundy.

162. United States Information Agency.
163. Agency for International Development before David Bell (formerly director of the Bureau of the Budget) took over in late 1962. Before Bell, Fowler Hamilton had been in charge.

Index